2017

George –

With fond memories of
our joint advocacy for
the entrepreneur – I hope
it continues to flourish
at Suffolk –

Carman

TOP PROBLEMS FACING COLLEGES

AND WHAT TO DO

by

NORMAN R. SMITH

PRESIDENT, ELMIRA COLLEGE
PRESIDENT EMERITUS, WAGNER COLLEGE
PAST PRESIDENT, SUFFOLK UNIVERSITY BOSTON
PAST PRESIDENT, RICHMOND AMERICAN INT'L UNIVERSITY LONDON
FORMER ASS'T. DEAN, HARVARD UNIVERSITY
GRADUATE SCHOOL OF EDUCATION
&
JOHN F. KENNEDY SCHOOL OF GOVERNMENT

TOP PROBLEMS FACING COLLEGES
AND WHAT TO DO

iUniverse books may be ordered through booksellers or by contacting:

iUniverse
1663 Liberty Drive
Bloomington, IN 47403
www.iuniverse.com
1-800-Authors (1-800-288-4677)

Because of the dynamic nature of the Internet, any web addresses or links contained in this book may have changed since publication and may no longer be valid. The views expressed in this work are solely those of the author and do not necessarily reflect the views of the publisher, and the publisher hereby disclaims any responsibility for them.

Any people depicted in stock imagery provided by Thinkstock are models, and such images are being used for illustrative purposes only. Certain stock imagery © Thinkstock.

ISBN: 978-1-5320-2247-0 (sc)
ISBN: 978-1-5320-2249-4 (hc)
ISBN: 978-1-5320-2248-7 (e)

Library of Congress Control Number: 2017906278

Print information available on the last page.

iUniverse rev. date: 05/01/2017

Norman R. Smith has logged 30 years, of his 45 years

in higher education, as a college and university president. Most recently, he has served as interim president at several institutions including Suffolk University Boston and Elmira College in New York. His first presidency was at Wagner College in New York where, during his 14 year tenure, the College evolved from bottom tier ranking and near bankruptcy, to full enrollment, fiscal stability, record fund raising, and top tier ranking. Smith went on to be President of Richmond The American International University in London, England and then became Founding Chancellor of what was to have been the largest American international university in the world, on the Egyptian Mediterranean coast west of Alexandria until that project ended following the "Arab Spring" revolution. Earlier in his career, he was Assistant Dean of two Harvard University graduate schools: Education and then the John F. Kennedy School of Government. He was a Fellow of the Harvard Philosophy of Education Research Center. He earned his doctorate from Harvard University and a BS & MBA from Drexel University where he launched his college career as Assistant Dean of Students, moving on to Philadelphia University as Vice President and Dean of Students. For additional background information and to contact, visit:

www.normansmith.org

iii

DEDICATED TO

Caroline Robinson Smith
Skidmore College '14
Rhode Island School of Design MFA Class of 2020

Dr. Susan Robinson
Skidmore College '73
Columbia University '75
Harvard University '84

Acknowledgments

I gratefully bow to my cherished friends and colleagues who have been inspirations and wise counsel during my professional life and/or the writing and editing of this book.

Walid Abushakra, Founder & Chairman, ESOL

Lord (Asa) Briggs of Lewes, Founding Chancellor, Open University UK
& Chairman of Governors, Richmond University London

Sir Graeme Davies, former Vice Chancellor, University of London
& Governor, Richmond University London

Richard Ekman, President, Council for Independent Colleges

Raymond Flynn, former Mayor of Boston &
US Ambassador to the Vatican

Tom Ingram, President Emeritus, Association of Governing Boards

George J. Matthews, Chairman Emeritus, Northeastern University

Robert Morris, Chairman of the Board, Elmira College

Chuck Pennoni, Chairman Emeritus, Drexel University

Richard Rosenberg, Chairman Emeritus, Bank of America
& former Trustee, Suffolk University Boston

Robert Sheridan, President Emeritus, Savings Bank Life Insurance
& former Trustee, Suffolk University Boston

Marshall Sloane, Chairman, Century Bank
& former Trustee, Suffolk University Boston

Donald Spiro, Chairman Emeritus, OppenheimerFunds
& former Chairman of the Board, Wagner College

Paul Ylvisaker, Dean Emeritus, Harvard Graduate School of Education

Graham Zellick, Former Vice Chancellor, University of London
& Chairman of the Board, Richmond University London

Dr. Christine Zaher

Principal Editor

PROBLEMS

Introduction

This book is written principally for private college presidents and senior officers, along with trustees, especially of smaller enrollment-revenue-dependent colleges. By private, I mean not-for-profit, independent colleges. My intention is to offer a compilation of problems that my experiences tell me should be in the forefront of their attention in their capacity as managers and leaders during a most challenging era in American higher education; a time when many colleges must change the way in which they have managed themselves for generations. In providing this compilation, I also hope to offer ways in which to redirect conventional thinking and behavior which will hopefully result in solutions.

My views are based upon personal experiences working on behalf of colleges and universities over the past 45 years. In more recent years, through the Registry for College and University Presidents, I have been intimately involved in the Board and Presidential activities of a number of private institutions where I have noticed recurring patterns of dysfunction largely based on conventional habits and routines that no longer work; or maybe never did work.

Some of the factoids and topics presented in this book were originally introduced in a book published five years ago, **WHAT COLLEGE TRUSTEES NEED TO KNOW**, co-authored with George Matthews, Chairman Emeritus of Northeastern University and Bryan Carlson, President of the Registry. That book was directed to Boards of Trustees while this one is intended also for senior officers. As such, readers of the former book may come across some familiar echoes.

Few will argue that the higher education landscape remains unchanged from what it was a generation ago. To the contrary, the changes over the last fifty years have almost completely transformed colleges and universities in ways that have left obsolete many of the managerial routines of the past.

More than any other factor contributing to this problem is the cost of attending college, especially private colleges and universities. Families are understandably opting for the college with the lowest price tag which is why most students, today, are enrolled in public universities and community colleges.

According to the most recent data disseminated by the Carnegie Commission and *The Chronicle of Higher Education 2015-16 Almanac*, there exist a little over 3,700 non-profit colleges and universities in the USA enrolling close to 19 million students. Another 1.6 million are enrolled in the nearly 1,500 for-profit and on-line institutions.

Of those 3,700 non-profit institutions, close to half are state-supported while the other half are independent, and heavily dependent on enrollment revenues.

Nearly 80% of non-profit college undergraduates today are enrolled in government-subsidized public universities like the SUNY system in New York State and the UC/CSU system in California. The remaining 20% or so, about 4 million undergraduate students, are enrolled in smaller sized colleges and universities typically identified as private or independent.

Fifty years ago, in the nineteen sixties and seventies, over two-thirds of all college students attended independent colleges and universities. Since that 'baby boom' college era, there has been a massive shift away from independent colleges toward state institutions for one inherently obvious reason: lower tuition rates offered by the multitude of state universities and community colleges that have been created over the past half century.

Among the 1,700 private colleges and universities, only 10% enjoy endowments of at least $500 million. Just 92 have endowments in excess of $1 billion. Seven have more than $10 billion and (no surprise) Harvard tops the list with $35 billion according to 2015-16 statistics reported by the National Association of College and University Business Officers (NACUBO).

In today's economy, the amount of revenue typically drawn from endowment is not likely to exceed 4% - 5%. Thus, even a seemingly impressive $500 million endowment isn't significant as the annual revenue spendable from such an amount contributes little more than $20 million to an annual operating budget that is probably at least five times larger, thereby leaving even 'comfortably endowed' institutions heavily dependent on annual enrollment revenues.

What is the point, you may be asking by now, of drowning you in all these factoids? Largely to help you understand why most college students and their families have, over the past half century, gravitated away from that half of non-profit colleges and universities that are tuition dependent toward public universities with large tax dollar subsidies that offer lower tuition rates.

The gap between public and independent/private higher education is significant.

The national average for public four-year tuition is about $8,000 a year and only $2,800 for public two-year institutions.

The average tuition rate, not counting room, board, books and miscellaneous expenses, among independent colleges is $28,300 (*Chronicle of Higher Education* 2015-16 Almanac).

Even those colleges that discount as much as 50% and sometimes higher, still leave financially needy students with having to pay the other half, at least $14,000 annually, along with as much as another $5,000 to $10,000 in additional costs.

The national median family income for 2015-16 is $55,313, before taxes meaning *at least HALF* the families in America cannot possibly set aside as much as $20,000 for even one child's annual college costs. Yet, at the same time, no college wants to close its door on any academically motivated student who cannot afford to pay private college tuition.

The 'inconvenient truth' is that there isn't an easy solution. Colleges have to pay employees, most of whom consider themselves underpaid as it is. Colleges are not exempt from utility bills. Classrooms equipped with state-of-the-art technology is expected by all students, regardless of how little they may be paying. The list of obligatory costs just keeps growing year after year.

This dilemma has many pundits forecasting the demise of many of the 1,700 heavily enrollment-revenue dependent colleges, especially those that continue to offer academic programs of little interest to the majority of college students and especially those institutions that, for all intents and purposes, 'sell' the product for less than it costs to make it. No such college can continue to over-enroll students who simply cannot afford to pay the necessary tuition rates. All colleges must face the responsibility that they must realize sufficient revenue to operate at an acceptable level of effectiveness.

Economic and social changes that have occurred, and continue to intensify, since the beginning of the new millennium, are jarring. The most striking changes include the following factoids, as reported in *The New York Times*, on May 12, 2012 *(in the feature "A Generation Hobbled by the Soaring Cost of College" written by Andrew Martin and Andrew W. Lehren)*:

American family wealth has dropped by 40% since 2007, and has returned to the wealth levels of the 1950s.

Nearly half (49%) of all college graduates since 2006 have not found a full-time job.

Nearly one-third of all adults under 30 years old are still living at home because they cannot afford to live on their own.

Over 48% of all college graduates owe more than $10,000 in student loans.

Since 2006, over two million students a year, who previously opted for a college degree, have shifted to vocational training schools to better ensure, they believe, that they will find a job upon graduation.

All this fundamentally explains why there has been a complete shift from independent private colleges to public 2-year and 4-year institutions. Most families today have concluded they cannot afford the high cost of private colleges.

The shift from private colleges to public ones has not yet significantly reduced the number of private colleges from the number that existed when they enrolled the most college students. Some prognost-icators, therefore, are predicting that many of these colleges, more than imaginable, will cease to exist. A frequently cited seer is Harvard Business School Professor Clayton Christenson who ominously foresees HALF of all private colleges failing within the next 15 years. *Christenson's prediction was recently cited in an Atlantic Monthly feature authored by David Wheeler in February 2017.*

The private colleges that will survive and flourish are those which understand these changes and are accordingly responding to them.

In their 2016 prognosis of higher education, Standard & Poor's succinctly summed up the state of U.S. higher education as being 'bifurcated.' That is, some private colleges and universities are doing better than ever before while others are digging themselves into financial holes they may never get out of.

The difference between being in 'the best of times' instead of 'the worst of times,' to cite Charles Dickens' way of describing bifurcation, comes down to financial sustainability.

Too many Boards of Trustees and Presidents have failed to come to grips with the high priority that economic realities should represent and which too often run counter to ideological norms that have ruled higher education standard practices for generations.

As the old saying goes, "the fish stinks from the head down." And, sure enough, those colleges in the greatest trouble are too often dysfunctional at the Trustee and/or Presidential level.

As you read on, which I hope you will want to do, note that we will not be in the position to name names for reasons we trust you can understand. Many of the problems cited were discovered at numerous different colleges with which we were engaged.

Unfortunately, I will too often be unable to cite the names of institutions being used as case studies for problems as the legal implications make doing so very prohibitive in today's litigious society. More about that 'problem' to come.

Norman Smith

NORMAN R. SMITH

THOSE WHO
REJECT CHANGE
ARE
THE ARCHITECTS
OF DECAY

UK PRIME MINISTER HAROLD WILSON

Preface

Today's Student Generations

Throughout this book, there will be references to the Millenniums and Generation Z, both unscientific groupings commonly used to characterize today's younger generations. These groups are cited mainly when making reference to the challenges they face in their lifetimes; challenges that colleges and universities must address perhaps differently than in the past. The world is changing as rapidly as Alvin Toffler predicted in his 1970's book, *Future Shock*. As the world changes, so must colleges and universities.

While there are varying characterizations of the Millennials and Generation Zs, a useful reference piece was published in *The New York Times* on September 15, 2015, entitled "Move Over Millennials. Here Comes Generation Z."

Written by Alex Williams, the article describes the Millennials as "self-involved, brash, narcissistic and entitled." For millennials, the birth range is typically set as somewhere between those born in the early 1980s to those born in the early 2000s. Based on that range, today's college freshman nears the end of the Millennial generation and we are, therefore, less than a decade away from having graduated all of this generational cohort.

Since about 2004, all new-borns have begun to form what is being described as "Generation Z." This group is described in the Williams article as being quite different from Millennials. They are "conscientious, hard working, anxious, mindful of the future and true digital natives." This generation will start enrolling in college in the early 2020s.

As both groups will be referenced in sections of this book, it seemed that this prefacing definition might help make those references easier to understand.

TOP PROBLEM #1

Board of Trustees Composition

U nlike corporate boards of directors, college trustees are unpaid volunteers. As such, their willingness to serve can justifiably be regarded as selfless and noble, which is very often the case. That said, there too often can be 'volunteers' who seek a college trusteeship for the wrong reasons and bring little to the Board of Trustees that is needed by the college.

Also, there is no one-size-fits-all formula for Board composition. The most suitable characteristics for Trusteeship depend on the state of the college and where it lies on the 'bifurcation' continuum cited by Standard & Poor's, as described in the Introduction to this book. Heavily endowed, full-to-capacity private colleges have very different needs than heavily tuition-dependent colleges, especially those facing or experiencing enrollment declines.

As this book is focusing on "Top Problems" facing colleges, the ideal Board characteristics emphasized herein will be based on the needs of the latter colleges which, to a large degree, comprise the majority of the approximately 1,700 private colleges in America.

These heavily enrollment-revenue-dependent colleges, which together enroll as few as 20% of all undergraduates, as noted above, have been adversely affected by the migration of college students to community colleges and state universities over the last half century.

Because of this migration, private, minimally-endowed colleges need to focus the majority of their attention on financially sustainable strategies. A wrongly composed Board of Trustees can, and often does, deflect and/or inhibit this vital focus.

Over the past 50 years, many Boards have emphasized the importance of egalitarian representation, partly in the name of diversity and largely in the spirit of shared governance. While a noble ideal, such a Board of Trustees can find itself overpopulated with special interest members whose individual advocacy can often take precedence over what is best for the overall future sustainability of the college.

Special interest advocacies are many. Most typical of college Boards are representatives from the faculty, from the student body, from religious orders and from the community.

Often, such representatives fill seats that are set aside and designated to represent such special interest groups.

This sort of composition understandably strikes many as conforming to the ideals of democracy as may well be the case. The obvious downside is that these constituent Trustees will often feel compelled to base all their decisions, and votes, on the beliefs and positions of the group they represent which is not always what is best for the institution as a whole.

Not infrequently, the popular ideal is not the best decision that has to be made and, conversely, the best decision is not always the most popular.

The best Trustees, therefore, are those who commit themselves to maintaining an objective distance from special interests which thereby enables them to make decisions that, in the long run, best serve the institution even when some affected groups don't get what they want.

Many, and perhaps even most, private colleges must confront the reality that they cannot do everything that everybody wants done. They cannot be all things to all people. They have to decide how they can realistically be financially sustainable which is only be possible as long as they remain enrollment-revenue-dependent . . . and only if they can find enough students with the wherewithal to pay tuition.

Therefore, the Board has to be composed of members who universally recognize that everyone

cannot have everything and, most importantly, **no**
Board of Trustees should put any advocacy
group's demands ahead of the best interests
of the college's longer term sustainability.

Unfortunately, Trustees holding seats reserved
for a subgroup will almost always put the interests of
that subgroup ahead of all else and, for that reason
alone, shouldn't be Trustees.

Special interest groups, like students
and faculty, should certainly be heard by
Trustees, but they shouldn't have a vote.

The same should be the case for religious order
representatives and elected officials concerned about
the effect of the college on the community. In each
case, to paraphrase John F. Kennedy, such advocacy-
group-oriented Trustees will inevitably be drawn to
asking not what they can do for the College but rather
what the College can do for their constituency.

Every college, and especially those with financial
sustainability challenges, needs only Trustees who

never compromise what is best for the college's ability to flourish and to serve its mission and its students.

In addition to Trustees filling designated seats reserved for a specific constituency, another type of Trustee to avoid is one who expresses an intent to offer only his/her expertise.

While there might be rare occasions to seek unique expertise for unique situations, like, perhaps, a real estate developer who can help with the financially beneficial use of vast unneeded campus property, there really aren't all that many areas of expertise that can justify a special Trustee appointment for such a limited and unilateral use.

And, as conflicts of interest can potentially arise, it is probably better to bring in such expertise as a paid consultant than as a Trustee.

Independent professionals including insurance executives, accountants, doctors and lawyers are also of potentially limited value to the Board and such professionals can create conflicts of interest that are better avoided.

The best Trustees for a private, minimally-endowed, enrollment-revenue-dependent college are seasoned and successful professionals whose career achievements have earned them recognition and high regard among their peers, and who also have the wherewithal to 'give and get' for the college.

This prerequisite for Trustee membership is particularly essential for the majority of private colleges in America that face enrollment and financial sustainability challenges. Think Maslow's Hierarchy of Needs. The first and foremost needs are the physiological which, for humans, include breathing, eating, drinking and sleeping. Without these needs being fulfilled, nothing else matters.

When those basics are adequately satisfied, humans move on to the next level of needs which includes safety and security; namely, the confidence that basic needs will continue to be fulfilled, including good health and family security, in the future.

It is only after these first two levels of needs are assured that qualitative needs like self-esteem, achievement, respect of others, morality, creativity, and lack of prejudice begin to matter.

So it goes for colleges. Those institutions facing enrollment declines and financial deficits must focus almost exclusively on overcoming the basic physiological needs.

Not until a college can be confident of enrollment stability, revenue security and fiscal balance, should it move on to albeit important qualitative issues; for example, access for talented students irrespective of their financial wherewithal, along with other ideals including that of shared governance.

It is precisely when colleges find themselves coping with physiological and security challenges, that the Trustees must be composed and dominated by successful professionals whose experiences can contribute to solutions that take the college beyond Maslow's basic physiological and security needs.

MASLOW'S HIERARCHY OF NEEDS

Personal Facets   **THE HIERARCHY**   **Institutional Facets**

SELF-ACTUALIZATION

Morality, Creativity, Spontaneity, Lack of Prejudice

Successful student outcomes, Need-blind enrollments, Optimum Diversity, Selflessness

ESTEEM

Confidence, achievement, Respect of others, Respect by others

Strong academic reputation, Application rates that far exceed capacity

LOVE/BELONGING

Friendship, family, Intimacy

Positive institutional morale, High student retention rate, Sense of shared community

SAFETY

Job security, Roof over Head, Healthy, Minimal uncertainty Safety of family

Job security, Secure Financial Sustainability, Capacity NET enrollments

PHYSIOLOGICAL

Life threatening prospects, Financially ominous, Sleepless

Insufficient enrollments, Capital plant deterioration, Deficit spending,

From the bottom up, no level can hope to be successfully addressed or achieved until the level (s) below is (are) resolved/satisfied.

Trustees need to be enablers, and need to be willing to use their stature and access on behalf of the College. Effective Trustees are not only cheerleaders for the College, but magnets to others who can help advance the College. Any such accomplished person wouldn't be where they were if they also didn't have valuable expertise to share with the College and its leadership.

Easier said than done. **Ideal Trustees are few and far between, and are sought out by many non-profit Boards for the same reasons as colleges.**

Probably the best place for colleges to find such Trustees is among the alumni/ae. Colleges have a great advantage in possessing tens, or hundreds, of thousands of graduates who have spent some of the most formative and memorable years of their entire lifetime at their college. As the years go by, their youthful past memories often become that much more cherished and important.

Many successful people get to the point in their lives where they are drawn to leaving legacies and giving, sharing some of their success with the institutions that shaped them. These kinds of Trustees can be worth their weight in gold, literally, and should be in the forefront of prospects for all private college Board of Trustees.

Successfully recruiting and retaining such Trustees, though, requires that their Board experience is worth their investment. Most such people don't have the time, or the tolerance, to suffer fools gladly and thereby waste their precious time.

Thus, an assemblage of peer Trustees who were brought on because of counter-productive principles like advocacy representation can result in losing those very Trustees who are in the position to do the most good for the college.

Every college has to have at least a half dozen distinguished graduates who, in turn, should be at the top of the Trustee prospect list if they are not already members of the Board.

If a college can recruit even one such superstar alumus/a to join the Board, he/she becomes a magnet for peer Trustees. *'You are the company you keep.'* Therefore, whoever leads the Trustees will often enable, or deter, the building of a strong and productive Board.

There are many examples of how distinguished alumni took leadership trustee positions and built powerhouse Boards that greatly advanced their colleges. At the top of the list is what alumni like Lawrence Tisch, Norman Stern and John Kluge enabled for New York University, a once urban commuting school that today reportedly receives more applications annually than Harvard.

A more recent example of a smaller college success story enabled by successful alumni can be told about Wagner College in the Staten Island borough of New York City. Wagner nearly closed in the mid-1980's after years of enrollment declines and operating deficits.

At nearly one-minute-to-midnight, a 1949 graduate of Wagner stepped in as a Trustee. He was Donald Spiro, a founder of OppenheimerFunds who, at that time, was Chairman and CEO. He took over the chairmanship of a Board that was populated with well-intended Trustees who had offered little more than their 'expertise,' which hadn't helped all that much. To their credit, the Board leadership willingly turned the chairmanship over to Spiro recognizing the value of what he brought to the table. Spiro's stature as Board Chairman completely transformed the College.

At his first Board meeting after becoming Chairman, Spiro announced that the Board would operate under the "THREE-G" principle. That is, **all Board members would be expected to 'give,' 'get,' or 'get off.'** Close to a dozen trustees soon thereafter chose option three.

That exodus was fine with, and fundamentally intended by, Spiro. He served as the magnet that drew another group of Trustees who, like him, were prominent and successful professionals: Phil Dusenberry, CEO of BBDO advertising; John Myers, Chairman of GE Investments; John Lehmann, owner of Butterick-Vogue. Within four years, Spiro's "magnetic' presence drew in about eight major chief executives, most of whom were Wagner alumni who had not before been actively engaged.

Over the next decade, Wagner College experienced the best fund raising years in its history which enabled a transformation that took the college from the bottom tier of rankings to the top, culminating with a TIME magazine College of the Year accolade.

Wagner College wouldn't exist today had it not been for the Board of Trustees that Don Spiro's involvement enabled, as can be said for the even more impressive evolution of New York University.

In today's tumultuous times for private colleges, **Trustees most needed by enrollment-revenue-dependent colleges are ones who, in the blunt spirit of Don Spiro, can 'give' and/or 'get.'**

No other expertise can match, or even come close to, Trustees who can open doors that result in multi-million dollar support. Ambitious outcomes at that level require either access or personal wherewithal, or both.

Any Trustee Chair lacking six or seven figure wherewithal should readily be prepared, in the spirit of putting the needs of the college first, to step down and turn over the reins the moment their Don Spiro materializes.

Another institution (which must remain nameless) not so long ago found its Don Spiro but lost him almost as quickly. Like Spiro, he was a major, but now retired, chief executive of a multi-billion dollar corporation. And, he was an alumnus who had not been very actively engaged throughout the decades since his graduation.

After attending two Board of Trustee meetings, one where he was fundamentally dressed down by a trustee who brought her 'expertise' but nothing else, he resigned declaring that he didn't have the time or patience to waste with the current Board membership. With the resignation of this powerhouse was also lost the potential for uncountable millions of dollars in donations along with the stature he brought that no other current Trustee could come close to matching.

As colleges rise above the physiological needs level, the composition of their Board governance can and will probably change.

Colleges lucky enough to enjoy a condition that is well above the physiological needs levels of Maslow's model may well be able to justify leadership that is less focused on fiscal sustainability.

Until then, colleges need Presidents and Trustees who know how to get to those higher levels. Once financially sound, the Board can perhaps evolve to a more egalitarian model.

Until then, the Board, and especially the Board leadership, needs to be comprised of seasoned and successful 'stars' with the selfless wherewithal to lead by example, especially when it comes to those necessary THREE G's.

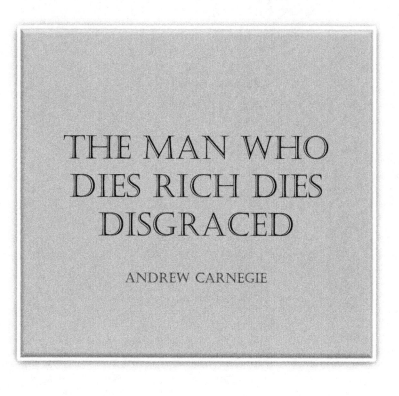

THE MAN WHO DIES RICH DIES DISGRACED

ANDREW CARNEGIE

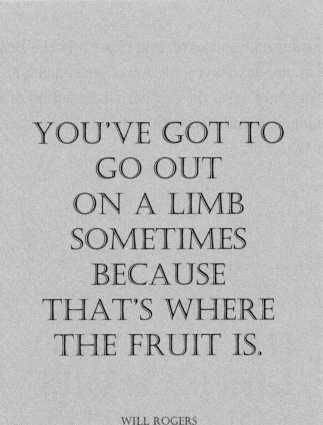

YOU'VE GOT TO
GO OUT
ON A LIMB
SOMETIMES
BECAUSE
THAT'S WHERE
THE FRUIT IS.

WILL ROGERS

TOP PROBLEM #2

Board of Trustees Micromanagement

S econd only to lack of prior presidential experience, a not uncommon problem in higher education is the all too frequent phenomenon of what is typically called Trustee micro-management. Too many college trustees don't understand where the lines of authority are drawn and therefore can make it impossible for the president to be the president. Such excessive involvement is usually cited as part of the Board's fiduciary responsibility (fiduciary wrongly interpreted by some Trustees as meaning anything with a financial obligation).

Thus, many Trustees take fiduciary responsibility to mean overseeing every nickel and dime being spent, thereby seeking Trustee involvement in every decision and action that has a cost attached to it. That, in turn, ends up being EVERY decision and action, period, as there are few activities at a college that don't have some sort of cost implication attached.

College trustees do indeed carry a fiduciary responsibility, one which even has legal liabilities attached to it. Trustees are the overseers of the College and thereby carry a legal burden of responsibility.

But, the trustee role is nevertheless limited. They essentially set policy and direction, as prepared and presented for approval by a management team headed by a president. While they have the prerogative to approve or reject such proposals, including the annual budget, trustees are stepping beyond the bounds of their responsibility when they look over management shoulders and attempt to manage the daily routine of executing policy and approved budgets. That responsibility is in the hands of the president whose job can be severely impaired by such Trustee intrusion.

Excessive Trustee involvement in management decision making and oversight is all too commonplace in higher education, particularly when the Board is heavily populated with Trustees who have volunteered their expertise and little else, thereby obligating them, in their minds, to exercise their expertise by engaging in management.

A significant part of the problem stems from the way in which the Board is typically sub-divided into committees that functionally align, more often than not, with the way in which the management of the college is organized.

There is a finance committee, of course, and the college CFO is typically the staff liaison to this board committee. The Provost is liaison to the Academic Affairs committee. The Enrollment Management VP is liaison to the Admissions Committee. And so it goes for Fundraising and Development, Athletics, Student Affairs and sometimes even schools like business, or nursing, or the arts.

All too often, the Trustee chairs of these subcommittees presume that their chairmanships make them responsible for the functional routine of the college area of activity they oversee. In doing so, they develop a relationship with the staff liaison that has that vice president or dean feeling that they are reporting to the Trustee committee chair rather than to the president.

On far too many occasions, for example, CFOs have admitted that they consider themselves to be reporting to the Trustee Finance Chair rather than to the President. This is especially a problem when the CFO and the President disagree on budget allocations. The CFO can then 'confidentially' appeal to the Trustee Chair and prevail over the president.

When a Trustee Finance Committee chair gets too close to the CFO, and vice versa, the president and the rest of the management team can be closed out of budget approvals. Instead, the CFO and the Trustee chair can control staffing and budget needs to a degree that subverts presidential leadership and effectiveness.

Some CFOs have managed to evolve into virtual CEOs as all vice presidents and deans redirect their affinity to where the financial decisions get made.

One Trustee finance chair, at a university that must remain nameless, went so far as to demand a review, which he handled personally, of all credit card charges. In conducting the review, he personally audited all credit card stubs and, in doing so, discovered several hundreds of dollars charged by one administrator for donuts. He ordered the CFO to cancel the credit card privileges of the user, who turned out to be a student affairs officer who had bought the donuts for a weekend student government leadership retreat. Obviously the Trustee should never have become involved at that level.

Another Trustee who was Chair of a (also nameless) university's Board Development Committee took it upon himself to fundamentally direct the development staff to the extent that the Vice President for Development, and his entire staff, saw themselves as unilaterally accountable to the Trustee Chair. A new president, upon encountering this arrangement, observed that the total cost of the fundraising operation, including staff salaries, exceeded the annual giving realized by over $2 million and thereby sought to reduce the gap by downsizing. The Development Vice President appealed to the Trustee Chair who intervened condemning the President for meddling with 'his' Development staff and demanding that the President deal with the Development personnel through the Trustee Chair. Once again, this particular Trustee had lost all sight of who was the chief executive and who wasn't.

Perhaps the best Trustees are those professionals who themselves are accountable to Boards of Trustees or Directors. **In the spirit of the Golden Rule (*don't do unto others what you wouldn't want done unto you*),** executives subjected to Board oversight are much less inclined to overreach when they themselves are on a Board. Rather, they understand the distinction between Board policy oversight and executive authority because of their own experience.

Boards of Trustees need to limit their role to hiring, evaluating and firing the president, thereby leaving the president free to execute the policies and budgets the Board has authorized. If the president fails to effectively execute the policies and strategies that were approved, and/or fails to abide by approved budget appropriations, then the Board can, and should, remove the president.

Undermining the president by turning a committee chairmanship into a position of executive authority is about the most destructive action that any Trustee can take.

A trustee also has to be vigilant of staff executives who seek to use a Trustee to overturn a presidential decision. This is no different than a child going to a grandparent to seek a change in parental mandate.

Trustees also have to appreciate that a college is a diverse and eclectic environment that is difficult to manage. Rarely, if ever, is there a unanimous consensus for anything.

If the Board invites faculty, students and staff to appeal their requests to the Board when they otherwise don't get what they want, the Board has effectively neutralized the ability of the president and his/her officers to manage the college. People by human nature always want to go to the top.

All college presidents face similar opportunities to undermine due process. If the president takes on every complaint brought to him/her, little else will be accomplished, not to mention the damage done to all other senior officers being circumvented, thereby making it impossible for anyone to do their job. As the president has to respect the authority of faculty to grade students and student affairs to sanction students for behavioral misconduct, the Trustees similarly have to stand behind the President and not intervene every time someone comes to them with a complaint.

Too many trustees just don't get this. They want to be 'involved,' so they say. They want to meet students and faculty so they can understand their needs and complaints, and then take them to the president for resolution. That is about the worst thing they could do although too many Trustees think, with the best of intentions, that is what they should be doing.

"I'm not interested in 'show and tell' at Board meetings. I want to be involved," is a frequent Trustee complaint, although much less frequent from Trustees who themselves have Boards to which they report.

Trustees have to come to grips with the fact that their role and authority does not include active engagement in the operations of the college. The only person at the college who reports to the Board is the president. Any trustee who actively interacts with subordinates of the president that, in turn, leads to them taking advocacy roles for that subordinate's agenda is subverting the ability of the president to be the president. This is a very fine line that needs to be trodden with care and is especially complicated when such subordinates challenge the president's management ability.

In cases where such doubts arise, Trustees will make a bad situation worse by intervening in a way that has presidential subordinates bypassing the president and dealing directly with trustees and Board committees before they proceed with presidential directives.

Trustees with doubts about presidential effectiveness should take those concerns to the Chair of the Board, who should, in turn, deal with the president directly and, if necessary, through Board processes established to review presidential performance and, when necessary, terminate the president.

Any trustee permitting faculty, students or administrators to use them as an alternative source of authority are contributing to institutional chaos.

Trustees should never give the college community a sense that they are prepared to overrule the president and that anyone with a complaint about the president should bring the complaint to them.

To the contrary, **it is critical to institutional effectiveness that the Board of Trustees stand behind the president even if they don't always agree with the way in which the president is proceeding.**

If, however, disapproval justifiably prevails, then the Board should use its authority to get a new president. While never a pleasant circumstance to confront, terminating the president is much better for institutional health than a Board that takes over the presidential role inviting the college community to deal directly with them rather than with the president.

The Board chair has to take a lead in ensuring that all Trustees understand the limitations of their authority and their role.

Too many Board chairs wrongly view their role as a convener of a 'decision by popular vote' assemblage. While it may be that policy decisions are determined by constitutional majority, the Board chair has a responsibility as a leader to guide those policy decisions and to collaboratively support the President.

One particularly dysfunctional college Board was heavily populated by well-intended professional retirees who lived in the neighborhood of the college. Several would take daily 'constitutionals' onto the campus randomly engaging faculty, students and staff in "how are things going?" conversations that typically included "how is the president doing?" One such trustee took it upon himself to serve as a pseudo 'inspector general' of campus facilities. Whenever he came across anything that appeared to be in need of repair, he would telephone the campus grounds manager and direct him to get someone over immediately to repair the problem.

Another such dysfunctional trustee, not retired, was a graduate of the professional school to which she was appointed as Trustee Subcommittee Chair. She took it upon herself to be the school's 'champion' which the Dean of the school encouraged. They would meet so frequently to strategize advocacy agendas that the Dean admitted he more frequently met with the Trustee Committee Chair than he did with the president and provost combined.

Yet another Trustee, an alumna with no professional credentials, appointed herself to a previously non-existent Trustee Property Committee. The subcommittee was charged with overseeing campus aesthetics which she took to include picking paint colors for walls and furniture. She dealt directly with the physical plant director and the CFO who together permitted her to hire her favorite interior designer who, in turn, acquired $500,000 in custom made Italian leather furniture for a reception area.

Perfect furniture could have been obtained for 10% of that amount but the expenditure wasn't realized by the president until the transaction was irrevocable. The Trustee didn't offer to donate the amount as she was providing her expertise and only her expertise.

Board chairs have to prevent this kind of abuse by managing the Trustees, not just convening them.

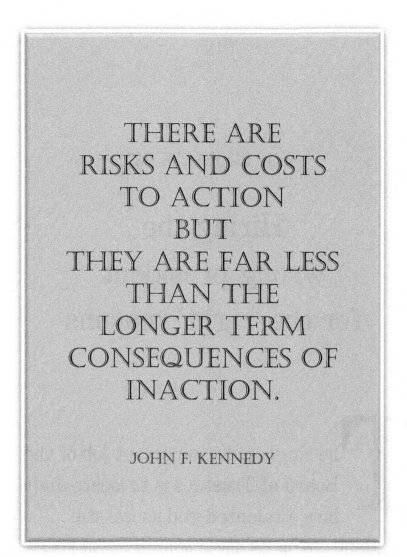

THERE ARE
RISKS AND COSTS
TO ACTION
BUT
THEY ARE FAR LESS
THAN THE
LONGER TERM
CONSEQUENCES OF
INACTION.

JOHN F. KENNEDY

TOP PROBLEM #3

Hiring the wrong president for the 'right' reasons

The single most important job of the Board of Trustees is to locate and hire a talented and successful **president**. To the detriment of many presidential hiring outcomes, Boards of Trustees have all too often turned over too much of this ultimate responsibility to the greater college community in the name of shared governance. In doing so, the results too often fall short of the vital needs of the institution.

While it rarely becomes public, far too many presidential hires are failures, largely because the processes in place to search and select college presidents are flawed.

Conventional wisdom dictates that presidents must be selected by popular consensus, not unlike the way in which we elect presidents, governors and mayors . . . too often with similar unsatisfactory results.

Conventional wisdom also opines that candidates be job applicants who are expected to fundamentally grovel for the job, campaigning among all affected constituencies from faculty, to students, to staff, to alumni, to the media, and others.

Conventional wisdom further insists that costly national searches, an ordeal that routinely takes a year, are the only way to find a suitable president.

Conventional wisdom too often leads to the selection of a president who may well manifest an array of positive qualities, but is fundamentally unqualified and underprepared to address the critical leadership and management needs of the institution.

A principal reason why this flawed process continues as standard operating procedure is that the failures never come to public attention. Boards of Trustees, along with shared governance search committees, will almost never let it be publicly known that their presidential search and decision was a failure. And, even if they were willing to acknowledge the error, they usually cannot make such an assertion without facing litigation from the 'failure' president who was probably terminated with a confidential agreement that neither party would ever reveal the truth.

The terminated president almost always agrees to resign, "for personal reasons," in exchange for what is often a massive and unearned compensation settlement. Part of the settlement invariably features an agreement that the Board of Trustees will not speak negatively of the failed president and the terminated president will not discuss the departure, or the college, in any way.

The only presidential searches cited are those where the institution was fortunate enough to be satisfied with the outcome, leaving all other colleges (in search of new presidential leadership) to believe that the standard year-long, national search is always a big success, and therefore the only way to go.

Boards of Trustees at any college faced with enrollment and financial sustainability challenges have to completely rethink the conventional wisdom approach to hiring a president. The president has to be someone whose skills and successes are in those areas of expertise that correlate to the specific vital needs of the institution which are not always in the headlights of eclectic search committee ideologies.

It is therefore important to realize that successful college executives are not likely to come begging for the job. Most, if not all, are comfortably ensconced in flourishing and productive leadership roles elsewhere and will have to be sought and even lured. To that end, it is the Trustees, and not the candidate, who will have to grovel.

The conventional search model in place is almost completely contrary to the way in which the best presidents are likely to be found. As a result, more often than not, most candidates who are willing and able to participate in such searches are limited, at best, to provosts and deans.

While there are many provosts and deans who have become exemplary presidents, the best examples of such outcomes are at colleges and universities fortunate enough to have minimal enrollment and financial challenges. Such fortunate institutions are better suited for presidents drawn to qualitative issues, like curriculum development, that are also more within the comfort level of provosts and deans.

NYU's Provost, Jay Oliva, for instance, succeeded John Brademas as President. Then, John Sexton, NYU's Law School Dean succeeded Jay Oliva. Neither presidential appointment required a national search. Those academic successions worked in part because NYU had already established itself as a flourishing and sustainable institution by the time Oliva, and then Sexton, had taken over.

Then again, Oliva and Sexton were exemplary financial managers and fund raisers too. That they were internal, each fundamentally groomed for future presidencies, represents an ideal model if the institution is fortunate enough to have talented and proven internal executives within the institution, that both Oliva and Sexton proved to be.

The biggest flaw with national searches, as already noted, is that successful 'sitting' presidents won't (because they can't) expose themselves to such public events that are roll-of-the-dice undertakings. The only 'sitting' presidents likely to throw their hat into that kind of ring, so to speak, are those presidents who are not succeeding where they are.

Most flourishing presidents are not going to risk everything they have for the prospect of moving on to a college, especially one challenged with enrollment declines and financial struggles. Their interest will be further diminished if they are expected to submit job applications and hence be revealed to the public, including their current employer, as candidates and applicants elsewhere.

An equally significant flaw with year-long searches is that the egalitarian search committees too often aren't qualified to pick the right president for the right reasons.

Many of the committee members don't even know what the 'right reasons' are.

The obligatory job description is usually constructed by the search committee and invariably looks like every other presidential job description at every other college.

The faculty representatives on the committee almost always seek a president who is, or has been, one of them. Someone who is a scholar; who has taught; who has published. And, for sure, someone who will protect the sacred cow tenets and rights of "the Academy", including tenure and sabbaticals.

The students want someone who 'cares about' students; who attends student events; who is sensitive.

Everyone, to no surprise, wants someone with the proverbial and charming sense of humor; and someone who is an 'effective communicator.'

Such committee-assembled job descriptions can run on for pages often minimizing the most essential managerial talents and track records.

All aspirants must then submit themselves as job applicants which includes writing a letter telling the committee why they want the job and in which ways they are qualified in all the job description criteria, including how well they walk on water.

At this point, the process has pretty much closed the door on virtually all of the prospective presidents most suited for and needed by the college.

Sitting presidents are just not going to risk their current job to publicly declare their desire to be elsewhere. They may as well be caught cheating on their spouses.

And, since the final vote will be popular, and therefore totally unpredictable, perhaps the person with the best sense of humor, or some other equally desirable but non-essential quality, will prevail, *which too often turns out to be the case.*

This conventional process also too often takes the decision away from the Trustees, who have effectively delegated their most important responsibility. At best, they can maybe insist that the search committee give them two or three unranked choices. Invariably, the final three invariably end up ranked anyway but it hardly matters as all three can fall far short of the institution's most essential leadership needs. The ideal candidates never emerge in the process because they never applied in the first place. The finalists, therefore, can too often have no relevant track record in the very challenges most in need of being addressed.

While there are many examples, as already acknowledged, of provosts and deans who have made great presidents, there are just as many, if not more, who have failed. The failures, however, rarely surface as already explained.

Any private college with enrollment and financial challenges needs a president whose expertise is, first and foremost, in areas of branding, marketing, sales, budget control, cost effective systems, and other such operational necessities.

Most provosts and deans have skills in curriculum, faculty development, professional development and accreditation.

The 'provost' counterpart in a hospital is someone comparable to the chief of surgery. This very talented professional is probably the best medical doctor at the hospital. Being President of the hospital, however, is a very different job than medical surgery, as it instead requires skills involving operating budgets, personnel and legal issues, and, often, major fund raising.

The same analogy applies to an airline company. The chief of pilots, who is an exemplary flier for sure, isn't necessarily likely to know anything about the business of running the airline.

The head curator of a museum is that institution's provost. While the curator is an expert in the museum's collection, the President of the museum runs the business of the museum which the curator not only is unlikely to know, but may not even be interested in knowing.

Most provosts and deans have probably never once had to think about marketing and branding a college, or selling an expensive college to prospective students and their families. Many have had little experience fund-raising and just as many don't like doing it and are not good at doing it.

But provosts and deans can be charming, and are almost always articulate and erudite. They have had to deal with the politics of faculty management which does require people skills. As such, they can often win the affections of search committees dominated by faculty and students.

The best president for a college challenged with enrollment and financial issues, though, is someone who understands that a private college today is a very expensive consumer product that 80% of college bound families cannot afford or are disinclined to 'buy.'

While all colleges understandably aspire to admit all talented students without regard for their ability to pay, at least 70% of private colleges in American cannot afford to enroll critical masses of non-paying students. The best presidents have to traffic that mine field, while aiming the college to higher plateaus where enrollment and finances no longer prevent the college's momentum.

Once again, those best presidents have to be recruited through a process that requires the Trustees to do the selling, not the buying.

As already noted, most of the best presidential candidates are likely to be productively and happily employed elsewhere. As such, they probably are not even keeping on top of job opening announcements because they aren't seeking to leave their current job.

As explained earlier, presidential searches are unique and challenging, especially when the college is most in need of a president who has already been a successful president. Someone who is not in need of on-the-job training.

The problem is the process.

Unlike vice presidents or deans, sitting college presidents greatly jeopardize their current job if they choose to become a candidate elsewhere. And, if not their job, they jeopardize their future success in their current job if they are not selected.

Because most presidential searches are not confidential, most sitting presidents cannot offer their candidacy. As a result, the candidates likely to be the best presidents avoid the process and are thereby never even considered.

Colleges in need of presidents who have already been successful chief executives should undertake a recruitment effort that is different than the conventional process usually employed by most colleges and search firms.

First and foremost, the Board of Trustees should back away from conducting a process that calls upon candidates to become job applicants whose candidacy will become public once they are a finalist, and also from compelling them to make the case why they want the job and why they qualify.

Rather, the roles should be reversed and the Board should become the 'seller' instead of the 'buyer.' The task should become one of seeking out prospects with proven presidential experience whom the college needs more than the prospect needs the college.

Boards shouldn't be deterred from this effort because of the flood of applications that will inevitably be received upon announcing the position opening.

It isn't hard to attract candidates. But, it is very hard to realize suitable candidates because the inevitable flood of applications, that most presidential searches generate, will include precious few experienced and successful presidents, if any.

The problem that arises when considering these major shifts in presidential search protocol is how to get the college community to agree to a less inclusive process. Faculty, in particular, have come to consider their role in selecting a president to be an absolute and inalienable right. Other constituents in shared governance have similar notions of ownership.

While easier said than done, faculty and other such groups must somehow accept the consequences of dysfunctional, albeit inclusive, methodologies.

The college community, and most notably the faculty, have to buy into the reality that a non-confidential search process, which all year-long search committee undertakings are certain to become, will close

the door on the best and most talented prospects.

Many of the Ivy League universities select their presidents in highly confidential, and therefore minimally inclusive, processes. That is because all their top candidates are flourishing elsewhere and cannot, therefore, become known job applicants.

Enrollment-revenue dependent colleges need a president who can, proverbially, hit the ground running. One such solution that has been successfully employed by many challenged colleges is the appointment of an interim president, made somewhat unilaterally by the Trustees without a national search or a broadly-based selection committee.

While not widely publicized, hundreds of colleges and universities nationwide have found that the interim appointment option best provides them with seasoned executives who probably would never have applied on a full time basis but who, in many cases, stay on in an interim capacity for upwards of five years.

A good example is Manhattanville College in Purchase, New York. Back in 2011, Manhattanville was facing the end of a long presidential term and confronted many daunting enrollment and financial challenges common in these recent years among small, private colleges. The Board discerned a need for a president that had extensive experience. They opted for an interim appointment instead of conducting a 'national search' that would likely have resulted in candidates who, at best, were provosts or deans.

The Registry for College and University Presidents had referred several of their most seasoned candidates leading to the appointment of Jon Strauss as Interim President. Strauss' impressive career had included presidencies of Harvey Mudd College in California and of Worcester Polytechnic Institute in Massachusetts, both top shelf academic institutions. Earlier in his stellar career, he was Senior VP of the University of Southern California and Financial VP of the University of Pennsylvania.

Had Manhattanville elected to conduct a search, no one of Strauss' august background, including Strauss himself, would likely have thrown their hat in the ring. Strauss, like most interim presidents, is a senior statesman not in search of a job and certainly not a job at a college smaller than prior lifetime positions.

While originally intended as a short-term interim assignment, Strauss' positive impact was so valuable that his tenure was annually renewed for the next five years. By the time he departed in 2016, the College had been advanced in ways that most would agree could not have been possible without the extensive and impressive experience that Strauss brought to Manhattanville.

Interim appointments are a fast-track solution for most senior positions (vice presidents and deans) and are especially valuable to colleges facing daunting challenges that can be best resolved by professionals who have proven track records in the positions they assume. As a result, the interim appointment of senior officers has become as popular as interim presidential placements.

The rationale for going interim is tied to the increased likelihood of bringing in a veteran who has successfully 'been there, done that' instead of someone who is looking to advance their career. While the latter may well succeed, such a selection nevertheless may result in someone whose prior experience is not likely to have been appropriate for the job being assumed.

In financially vital positions like chief development officer or chief enrollment officer, the 'dream' hire would be someone who is widely acknowledged as having been very successful at an institution that the hiring institution would want to emulate. Anyone that successful is not likely to be interested in a comparable position at a comparable institution, and especially a challenged one.

Therefore, most applicants to such positions will bring only more junior experience, albeit perhaps successful experience to date. But, hiring such an unproven candidate is a risk that might be successful but is not as assured as opting for more senior and accomplished veterans available as interims.

A major plus with interims is their typical immediate availability. National searches can take most of a year, leaving the institution without needed leadership for what could be a critical time when results are needed quickly. Interims are typically ready to begin within weeks, sometimes even days, of being tapped. And, like presidents, interims at all other levels are typically top shelf veterans who would not likely be among the pool of applicants seeking the job through search firms and advertisements.

Most important, on-the-job training is not needed by veteran interims.

They are at a point in their career where they are no longer looking to advance themselves to higher level jobs or institutions. In most cases, they have probably already had successful runs at institutions that might be construed as more prestigious than the ones they join as interims.

And that is where the institution wins. They bring on senior statespersons who bring with them the best practices of their profession, which is why such interims are often called upon to stay for years. Then, when all is Presumably ticking like a Swiss timepiece, a truly permanent appointment can be made.

NORMAN R. SMITH

TOP PROBLEM #4

Apologizing for
private college cost

W ith only 20% of all college
students now attending private
colleges, price has clearly
become the primary consideration among
most college-bound families. Colleges losing
enrollments and revenues because of this too often

apologize for high costs and attempt to win back the other 80% by portraying themselves as less expensive than meets the eye.

Some colleges have even increased their scholarship offers to a level where they are realizing as little as 30% of the tuition rates they are advertising. In doing so, they may be bringing in students, but they aren't bringing in the money they need to pay for the cost of educating them.

As many colleges are now learning the hard way, trying to compete with community colleges and state universities on a price basis is financial suicide.

There is no silver bullet, but there is certainty that any college selling the product for more than it costs to make it is going to cease to exist.

The only solution may well be to successfully make the case that the price of your college is fair and that one gets what one pays for.

The 20% of families that remain drawn to the more expensive private colleges and universities is heavily represented by those fortunate enough to be in the position to afford the cost of private education for their children. Parents in this cohort are themselves usually college educated and thereby value the benefits of a quality college experience which, they perceive, prevails in the private colleges and universities.

Also noteworthy are the many affluent families who send their offspring to public universities because they are unconvinced that private colleges are worth the difference. These people need to be awakened.

Private colleges need to abandon attempts to portray themselves as being just as affordable as public schools and instead make the case that they are worth what they cost. Further, that the cost is not out of line with the costs of other major investments today.

In other words, instead of being defensive, colleges should more assertively correct the misperception that private college tuition has outpaced the cost of everything else.

To the contrary, there is a case to be made that the relative cost of a college education has been wrongly exaggerated.

That is, most everything else we buy has increased in price over the past 40 years at a rate greater than college tuition. This is especially true when considering the actual cost paid by most students instead of the published rates more usually cited by the media.

Consider these comparisons:

	1975	2015	%
Median Annual Income	12,600	55,300	440%
Mercedes Benz roadster	20,000	90,000	450%
Gasoline per gallon	.59	2.20	370%
Pack of cigarettes	.45	8.00	1777%
New York Times newspaper	.30	2.50	830%
Average house	48,000	210,000	440%
Postage stamp	.13	.49	380%
Pound of coffee	1.12	8.99	800%
Loaf of bread	.28	2.35	840%
5 lbs of sugar	.65	2.84	440%
Movie ticket	2.00	9.00	450%
NYC apartment $/sq. ft.	45	1,100	2300%
Private college tuition	10,440	32,405	310%
Private tuition/room/board	16,140	43,900	270%

While independent college tuition is, without argument, higher than that of tax-subsidized public institutions, the inflation rate of private college tuition rates over the past 40 years is actually lower than most other increases, including income.

Tuition inflation is even lower when the average private college tuition discount rate, estimated at 40% of tuition, is factored in. By that comparison, private college tuition has actually lagged against many, if not most, other financial indicators.

At first glance, $43,900 for tuition, room and board comes across as a blindingly excessive amount of money that exceeds the after-tax net of the median annual income of $55,300. And that, once again, is why 80% of all college students are attending public institutions.

But consider that an annual college academic year runs about 30 weeks between September and June, taking out term breaks and other holidays, including between semesters. That comes to 210 days a year.

Taking the average 4-year tuition, room and board rate of $43,900, the daily college rate is $209.

Since the average discount on tuition rate is at least 40% and often more, the annual average tuition, room and board rate that most students pay is, usually, rarely higher than $30,000 making the daily college rate about $140.

While sources vary, $120 is typically cited as the national average cost for one night in a hotel room...no meals (as is included in the tuition, room and board rate that averages to $140 a day at the average college.)

The hotel rate also doesn't include college coursework that leads to a college degree. So, **for $20 a day more than the cost of an average hotel room, private colleges and universities are far from excessively priced.**

That doesn't mean private colleges are not expensive on an annualized basis. Admittedly, few reside in a hotel 30 weeks a year. That acknowledged, though, few also criticize the cost of a hotel room at $120 a night without food. So, is it reasonable to criticize $140 a day for room, three meals . . . *and a college education thrown in for good measure?*

What private colleges need to convey more effectively is that families shouldn't abandon the prospect of attending an independent college because it is too expensive.

Easier said than done, perhaps, and especially for those families who cannot afford it. But that is why most college students are now in community colleges and state universities. Nothing can change that. However, those same public institutions are heavily enrolled with the children of families who can afford private college tuition. Those families need to be persuaded that the higher cost of a private college will be well worth it.

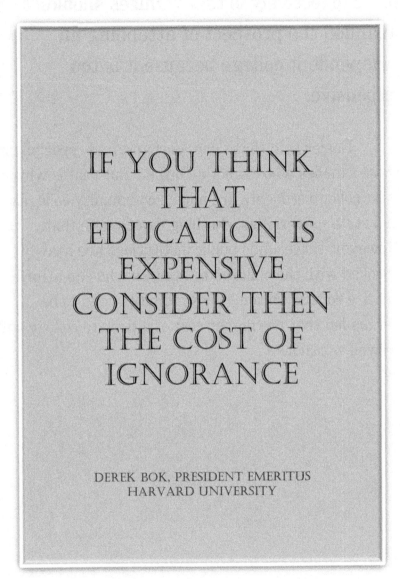

IF YOU THINK
THAT
EDUCATION IS
EXPENSIVE
CONSIDER THEN
THE COST OF
IGNORANCE

DEREK BOK, PRESIDENT EMERITUS
HARVARD UNIVERSITY

NORMAN R. SMITH

TOP PROBLEM #5

Selling the product
for less
than it costs to make

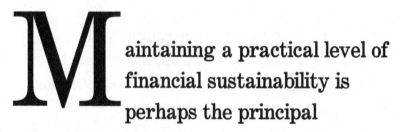aintaining a practical level of
financial sustainability is
perhaps the principal
prerequisite upon which all other aspects of a
strategic plan must be based. And, for today's
enrollment-revenue-dependent colleges and universities,
that underlying principle is perhaps the most daunting
and difficult.

The higher education enrollment landscape has completely changed over the past half century. In the early-to-mid 1960s, now over 50 years ago, most college students attended the 2,000 or so private colleges and universities that existed, and largely remain, in the US.

Then, in the late 1960s through the 1970s, the baby boom caused state governments to fund and build a massive collection of state universities and community colleges that today enroll most undergraduates.

Where the 2,000 or so private institutions once had over three-quarters of the enrollment market, those same number of private colleges and universities (give or take a few) remain but are now vying for only a quarter of the market they once controlled.

Many prognosticators have concluded, and they may well be right, that there are too many private colleges at this point for the number of students who seek a non-public college education.

More than any other reason, as already cited but nevertheless important to stress, the public institutions now own most of the enrollment market because their tuition rates are low, and cannot be matched by private colleges, thanks to the tax dollars they receive from their respective state governments.

With the exception of the marque colleges and universities, like the Ivies, most private colleges and universities have been struggling to maintain their past enrollments. Too many of these struggling institutions have employed strategies to draw in enrollments by increasing their 'scholarship' offers to levels that attempt to match the public university bottom line tuition rates.

The National Association of College and University Business Officers (NACUBO) long ago set 50% and above as unsustainable discount levels that, for all intents and purposes, force colleges to sell their product for less than it costs to make it. In doing so, such colleges are burying themselves in accumulated debt that will ultimately close them down.

Presidents and Trustees have to carefully monitor enrollment data that too often are rationalized in ways that make a bad situation look much better than it really is.

If not carefully scrutinized, enrollments can look up when they are, in fact, down.

Consider the following five-year bar-chart of enrollments that shows a 100 student increase from 1,100 students in the first year to 1,200 students in the fifth year. This steady growth obviously seems to be a sign of good health and momentum in every way.

WHAT IS WRONG WITH THIS CHART???

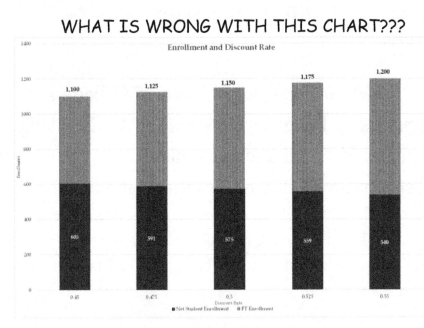

**Total Enrollment is up 100 students
But financial-equivalent enrollment is down by 55 students**

What also happened over that same five year span was that discounting increased at a rate of 2.5%

each year from 45% in the first year to 55% five years later.

When taking that high rate of tuition discounting into effect, a net equivalent enrollment is revealed that, contrary to a 100 student increase over five years, is really a net tuition equivalent student drop of 55 students from 605 students in the first year to only 540 students five years later.

Nothing is more important to an enrollment-revenue-dependent institution challenged financially because of enrollment shortfalls than to realize the difference between enrollment growth and NET enrollment growth. **The biggest mistake too frequently made by colleges seeking to improve their fiscal health is to build an enrollment headcount than can actually be a NET enrollment decline.**

It is easy to do. Simply keep increasing your scholarships in order to attract students which will concurrently decrease revenues while at the same time increase operating costs. Most of the private colleges in the most precarious condition got that way by thinking that enrollment growth was always better than not, as the previous bar chart reveals.

The full-tuition equivalent shaded bar, at, say, a published annual tuition rate of $30,000, shows that the 65 tuition-equivalent loss over five years (while 'boasting' a 100 total student increase) actually turns out to be a tuition-revenue loss of nearly $2 million annually. Moreover, the additional 100 students being heralded generate additional operating costs in a scenario where $2 million less is being realized as revenue.

Obviously, such enrollment "increases," which are much too frequently lauded as huge successes, are, to the contrary, disastrous.

Like it or not, and many don't like it, enrollment-revenue-dependent colleges have to think of themselves as an expensive consumer product in a market place where so much product exists that the paying customer has the pick of the litter. If that expensive consumer product is finally sold for less than it costs to make it because paying customers go elsewhere, then that particular expensive consumer product is going to eventually disappear from the marketplace.

Enrollment-revenue-dependent institutions have few options except to draw critical masses of students from the 20% of college bound families having the financial wherewithal to pay for at least 50% of the posted full-tuition rates.

The only alternative, albeit daunting and out of reach for many small colleges, is to build a massive nine-figure endowment that generates enough investment income to offset tuition-revenue shortfalls resulting from tuition discounts that exceed the 'red-line' NACUBO 50% level.

Few colleges among the 2,000 or so independent institutions still operating have any realistic hope of an endowment in the hundreds of millions. To survive, these institutions must find and retain paying customers.

On the hopeful side, the low-cost lure of public universities may eventually overcrowd them to the point where families able to afford private higher education will return there. Already, many public universities are overcrowded resulting in over-enrolled courses often making it impossible for students to complete the courses necessary for graduation.

Governor Andrew Cuomo of New York State recently enacted free-tuition for any student whose family earns less than $125,000 a year. The program takes effect immediately for the Fall of 2017 with a first year family earning ceiling of $100,000 that will be increased to $110,000 in 2018 and $125,000 in 2019. Some are already declaring the New York program as the beginning of a national trend, which while a meaningful step toward insuring access to college for all, could at the same time be a further overcrowding of public universities.

While some are seeing free public higher education as the beginning of the end for enrollment-revenue-dependent private colleges, that overcrowding could make public universities less attractive to many.

Public universities have significant enrollments of students from affluent families. Many affluent parents see low state university tuition as a tax break they have earned, thereby offering their children an automobile, as one metaphoric example, for the money saved by attending a public university.

But, if free tuition increases enrollments at already overcrowded public universities, many families may finally recognize the value of sending their children to less crowded private colleges where their son or daughter may well have a greater chance of academic success. Time will tell.

In the meantime, though, private colleges will continue to heed the need to maintain financial sustainability as there is no way they can successfully emulate free public universities and hope to survive.

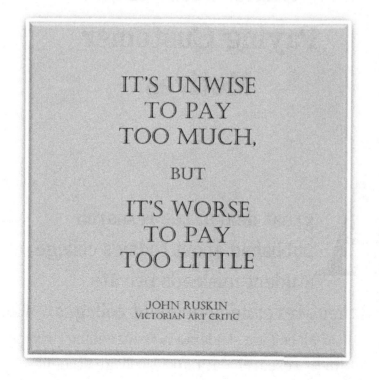

IT'S UNWISE
TO PAY
TOO MUCH,

BUT

IT'S WORSE
TO PAY
TOO LITTLE

JOHN RUSKIN
VICTORIAN ART CRITIC

TOP PROBLEM #6

Understanding Paying Customer Motives

A great deal of the research published about today's college student misleads private enrollment-revenue-dependent colleges. With only 20% of all college students now attending private colleges, most research data about college student

80

trends are heavily dominated by the perspectives of the 80% who opt for public universities and community colleges. As such, too little research emerges about the 20% of students most likely inclined toward private colleges and instead emphasizes the motives of the 80% drawn to public institutions.

Enrollment-revenue-dependent colleges have to figure out a way to brand and market themselves based on the consumer traits that best reflect the perspectives of that 20% who are likely to opt for private colleges.

As already echoed many times in this book, price is the major reason why 80% of today's students are enrolled in public universities and community colleges, a near complete reversal from the 1960s. In response, private colleges continue to increase the size of their tuition discounts in order to sway consumer decisions in their direction. NACUBO reports that, in 2015-16, the national average tuition discount was 48.6%. If that was the average, obviously many private colleges are offering much higher discounts and setting themselves up for a financial catastrophe.

A 50% discount still leaves families with having to pay the other 50% which, in itself, far exceeds most state and community college rates.

Like it or not, private colleges have to construct a product image, including pricing, that appeals to the 20% of consumers with the financial wherewithal to afford private colleges.

Those families are heavily represented by parents who are college educated and whose family income and wealth are high enough to afford private college tuition. While these families may also be aspiring to pay as little as they can, their highest priority is the future of their children as measured by the quality of their education. To that end, they are not looking for the cheapest solution (as are 80% of families).

As Standard & Poor's wrote in their 2016 private higher education sector prospectus, many expensive private colleges are experiencing record demand and are having to turn away more students than they enroll.

This 'best of times' for marque colleges is the opposite of what other private colleges are experiencing because they are not among the colleges that the 20% of families view as having the quality that makes them worth the added cost.

Too many private colleges, in a mad scramble for the 80% of college-bound students, brand themselves as cheap or affordable. While that sometimes draws some curiosity from the 80% that may even lead to increased enrollments, it can concurrently deter applications from the 20% who can afford a private college.

College-educated, affluent parents seek bragging rights in addition to assurances that they are sending their children to a high quality private college. If a college brands itself as 'cheap and affordable,' it may actually be lowering its appeal to the very audience it most needs: families that can afford to pay.

Consumer behavior must also be taken into consideration. For generations, high price has correlated with quality whether warranted or not. In virtually all consumer products, buyers tend toward the most expensive product they can obtain for the best price they can get it. If that same product, though, had a lower retail price more in line with what most people actually pay, the product would be less desirable.

The inconvenient truth is that college tuition is part of that consumer syndrome. Families that can afford private tuition also enjoy 'bragging rights' that their child has obtained a scholarship. And, they equally enjoying paying less than 'retail.'

Similarly, high school college counselors advise all parents to negotiate, especially with those colleges not among the marque schools that are full to capacity.

This is a mine field that colleges have to tread through very carefully in order to avoid being perceived as desperate, or acquiescing to scholarship (discount) levels that exceed financial viability.

Some colleges have understandably concluded that such discounting and bartering is contrary to how a college should be engaged. In response, they have eliminated all such discounting practices and lowered their 'retail' prices to a level that they believe more honestly reflects the tuition rate that students are paying after discounts are applied.

That adjusted tuition level, as NACUBO has reported, can result in advertised tuition being half of what previously was posted.

While that price drop sounds like an irresistible 'deal' that should draw more customers, it may instead deter more customers than it adds. Time will tell.

A sobering lesson in this kind of consumer syndrome can be learned from JC Penney's failed strategy aimed at increasing their customer base. In late 2011, they hired the very successful Executive Vice President of Apple computer retail sales, Ron Johnson (BS Stanford, MBA Harvard). During his 11 year tenure at Apple, the company had experienced record-breaking sales without ever discounting their products. Upon arriving at Penney's, Johnson decided he would employ the same Apple retailing strategy. He eliminated all discounts and sales declaring that JC Penney products would be sold at 'fair and square pricing every day.'

What worked at Apple, probably because they had a product available nowhere else, completely bombed at Penney's. Less than a year after being hired, sales dropped 32% in one quarter marking what has been cited by some financial analysts as one of the worst quarters in retail history.

Ron Johnson was terminated less than two years after he was hired. He was replaced with the former JC Penney CEO who had been fired when Johnson took over. And, the discounts and sales are back.

Very few consumer products have successfully managed to maintain high pricing without ever offering a discount or sale. Apple is one. Tiffany, Louis Vuitton and Cartier are others.

With thousands of private colleges vying for the same 20% of the applicant pool able to afford private college tuition, the likelihood is low that any smaller college can defy the consumer appeal of scholarships and discounts.

What these colleges must be careful to avoid, though, is presenting those discount offers as a reflection of their 'affordability' Such a characterization can translate into 'cheap' and 'low quality' by those wanting the highest quality product, but with the highest discount.

Scholarships and discounts have to be presented in a way that does not diminish the quality of the institution as reflected, unfortunately in part, by its price.

Yes, I acknowledge that this kind of thinking does run contrary to the ideals of higher education, especially with respect to accessibility. As noted above, ideally, all students should have the right to attend the college of their choice without respect to their financial wherewithal. To think of a college or university as a consumer product subject to the whims of buyer motivation is viewed by many as appalling.

Unfortunately, these ideals run contrary to the survival of most enrollment-revenue-dependent colleges, all of which are at least 90% dependent on students and their families being able to pay tuition rates that far exceed what state and community colleges are able to charge because of tax dollar subsidies.

Such private colleges have to find paying customers and have to accommodate the factors they use to make their college decisions even if those factors defy logic.

Jerry Della Femina, an advertising agency icon of the mid-twentieth century, wrote a book about consumer quirks that serves to reinforce the necessity to heed the perceptions of buyers.

Two quick examples that resonate:

Johnson and Johnson spent years and vast amounts of dollars developing a first aid cream that worked wonders without stinging when applied. However, no one would buy it because the prevailing public perception was that such a disinfecting product had to sting when applied if it was going to work. J&J relented and added some alcohol so it would sting. The product was then successful.

Betty Crocker developed the perfect cake mix. They taste-tested the cake with the finest home-made ones and the box cake mix won every time. But, no one would buy it because all that had to be added was water. Consumers refused to believe that a cake mix could be that good with just water being added. So, Betty Crocker added the requirement of folding in an egg. The product was then successful.

Thus, while it seems logical, as it did to Ron Johnson at JC Penney, that lower prices every day would appeal to buyers, that is not necessarily the case if price is viewed as a reflection of quality. In that case, buyers would rather have the discount on the higher priced product which, because of its higher price, must be better.

Another clear example of idiosyncratic consumer behavior is the 20% discount coupon that has become the trademark of Bed, Bath and Beyond. The coupon has become so ingrained in consumer expectation that most BB&B customers will not patronize the store if they are without one of the coupons.

And so it goes, at least for the foreseeable future, with private colleges, especially those outside of the top marque schools like the Ivy League. All others, like it or not, probably have to continue to be priced at levels that enable large scholarships/discounts.

But, these same colleges have to exercise great caution to insure that the 'retail price' appears to reflect high quality and that the scholarship is not promoted as an affordable enabler.

As indicated above, a number of colleges experiencing enrollment challenges, like most private colleges everywhere really, have decided to defy the tenets of consumer behavior associated with the high tuition, high discount syndrome and instead are retracing the footsteps of JC Penney by eliminating all discounts in favor of a lower base tuition rate.

Two such colleges, both reporting success with this change of pricing, are Rosemont College on the Main Line of suburban Philadelphia and Utica College in the central New York Finger Lakes region. Both are in regions heavily populated with competing colleges, both public and private. Rosemont, most notably, is surrounded by prestigious national colleges that are flourishing. Nearby are Villanova University, Haverford College, Bryn Mawr College, St. Joseph's University and Swarthmore College, to name just a few. Utica is near a similar high density of institutions including Hobart & William Smith Colleges, Ithaca College, Syracuse University, Hamilton College, Skidmore College, Union College and a number of SUNY (State University of New York) campuses.

Utica dropped its tuition from $34,466 to $19,996 in 2015 taking effect Fall 2016. As their prior freshman discount rate had been 62%, their actual freshman tuition rate had, in reality, been about $13,100; much lower than the revised, no-discount, $19,996. So, if this change in pricing is favorably received, Utica could be realizing more tuition revenue than before.

Rosemont similarly dropped their combined tuition, room and board rate from $46,000 to $30,000. Their tuition rate has been dropped to $18,500. As the *Philadelphia Inquirer* pointed out in a media account chronicling this pricing change, "students save nowhere near $16,000 under Rosemont's new pricing structure" because past discounting pretty much matched the new pricing without discounting.

That said, both Rosemont and Utica report increases in applications, and modest increases in actual Fall 2016 enrollments that have both colleges concluding that this strategy is working for them.

However, some parents interviewed by the *Philadelphia Inquirer* seem to believe that they will be saving upwards of $50,000 when that just isn't the case with a pricing change that, at the bottom line, isn't in reality all that different.

As the newness of such practices settles in, it will be interesting to see what parent consumers finally conclude when they realize this. Then we will see to what degree conventional consumer behavior prevails.

In Rosemont's case, will families prefer paying $30,000 without 'scholarships?' Or will they be more drawn to a $46,000 college (comparable to the pricing at neighboring colleges like Bryn Mawr, Haverford and Villanova) that offers a $16,000 scholarship?

Conventional wisdom says that the latter will prevail as the more desirable as the higher price connotes quality (whether warranted or not) while the discount represents a 'bragging right' of having received a scholarship (whether it is or is not).

What Rosemont, Utica and other colleges are daring to do might someday be seen as a high road that eliminates the false perceptions, conveyed by discounts called scholarships, that today are a common practice. If such false perceptions. so common in typical consumer behavior. are dispelled, many other colleges might likely follow with enthusiasm.

The fundamental problem of higher tuition rates at private colleges, though, will not change. College bound families may well eventually become accustomed to the 'new normal' of lower price without any discounts, but enrollment-dependent institutions will continue to struggle for the same small applicant market.

Sign at Rosemont College's entrance

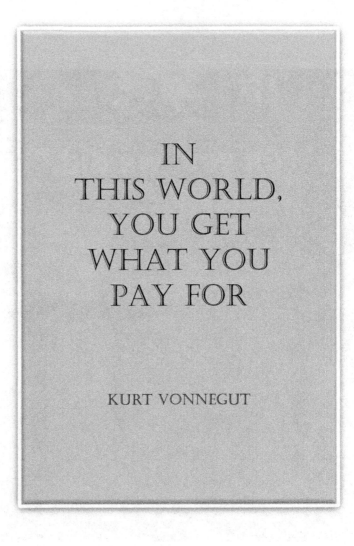

IN
THIS WORLD,
YOU GET
WHAT YOU
PAY FOR

KURT VONNEGUT

TOP PROBLEM #7

Managing
Instructional
Costs

nyone aspiring to become a college
president, provost or dean might
be well advised to make no
reference to the contents of this chapter,
especially when meeting with the typical search
committee that will be populated with faculty. And
therein lies the problem. Colleges are labor intensive

making personnel the most costly single element of the operating budget.

That being the case, personnel productivity, including instruction, needs to be critically assessed like never before, and, if and where found inadequate, is subsequently corrected.

At most colleges, though, instructional costs, especially those associated with full time faculty work obligations, are a sacred cow.

In the spirit of shared governance, curriculum development and delivery, along with related faculty work obligations, are heavily influenced by the full-time, tenured faculty along with national standards as monitored by the American Association of University Professors (AAUP).

As compared to virtually any other professional job in America, full time tenure college professors have a pretty attractive deal, beginning with the annual basic faculty workload .

Almost every college and university has a fall semester that usually begins in late August and ends in early to mid-December for a total of about four months. Then, there is a winter-spring semester which begins in early to mid-January and ends, usually, in mid-May for a total of another four months. These two semesters comprise the core obligation for many, if not most, full-time professors. Eight months!

The other four months include a three-month span between spring Commencement and the fall semester, along with a near full month between the two semesters of the academic year. During these months, professors view themselves as having time to conduct research and other scholarship that keeps them professionally current.

Many other professionals, including medical doctors, lawyers, pilots, *et al,* could also arguably make the case for comparable time to maintain their levels of competency but don't enjoy anything that comes close to four months a year.

Then again, many college professors might rightly contend that doctors and lawyers earn more.

In response, many colleges have limited the core faculty obligation in ways that provide professors with supplemental pay for just about anything not associated with instructional obligations. Being on committees, showing up for admissions open houses, and even student orientation provide extra pay at some colleges.

It may not be possible to do anything about all this, but the **one area that college presidents and provosts should be monitoring is courses being offered as they relate to the needs of students.**

In too many cases, faculty-run academic programs have evolved over the decades to meet the needs and preferences of faculty rather than students.

Common disservices to the needs and preferences of students include:

1. Too many courses offered mid-week in mid-day hours, a favorite period of time that permits faculty to avoid teaching on Mondays and Fridays, thereby providing four-day weekends.

2. Evening courses once-a-week are too often favored by faculty with second jobs, like accounting professors with private practices.

3. Inadequate numbers of core courses so that professors can teach courses of professional interest to them. Understandably, faculty get bored teaching the same courses semester after semester, year after year, decade after decade, even though each new year brings in new students in need of the same basic courses.

Routines like the ones cited above can result in students having difficulty getting into the courses they seek and need while concurrently being faced with taking courses they don't necessarily want at times that are not in their best interests.

Another major problem is that many such unattractive and unneeded courses are also grossly under-enrolled. All this can result in instructional costs far exceeding practical levels and, in many cases, not even paying for themselves.

As the financial sustainability of enrollment-revenue-dependent colleges becomes a survival issue, such problems have to be confronted and corrected.

A useful starting point would be to at least study the degree to which full time faculty are carrying a financially realistic student teaching load.

The conventional standard teaching load at undergraduate colleges has long been eight courses per full time professor per academic year. At most colleges, this breaks down to four courses in the fall semester and four courses in the winter-spring semester.

Let's then assume 15 students per course as an average standard acceptable to most as a good teaching environment.

Eight courses per professor with an average of 15 students each would give a full time professor an annual student teaching load of 120 students.

Many college professors carry annual student teaching loads that far exceed 120. Popular teachers offering core required courses can often carry loads that are well over 200.

What startles many college executives when looking at this for the first time is the number of professors whose annual student teaching load doesn't come anywhere close to 120. That these data, when known to faculty, also startle, if not alarm, those professors with 200+ student teaching loads.

Also revealing is the frequency with which some of the most senior, and highest paid, faculty have the smallest student teaching loads.

Such performance standards can be, and often are, resisted quite assertively by faculty. Such standards, however, must increasingly be addressed especially by those financially challenged private colleges which have little choice but to operate more cost effectively. The solutions should ideally be collaborative, inclusive and operate within faculty governance systems.

Even faculty can sometimes agree about levels of productivity when gross underperformance is brought to their attention. At one large urban university, for instance, senior tenured faculty were so minimally monitored that one of the highest paid veteran professors had managed to reduce his fall campus presence to Tuesdays and Thursdays from 1 p.m. to 5 p.m. Additionally, the most senior faculty had somehow managed to reduce their annual teaching obligation to five courses a year.

This particular veteran, over 30 years in tenure and earning well over $200,000 annually, taught two courses in the fall and three in the spring. The two fall courses were taught back-to-back on those two days and both courses were exactly identical. In this one fall semester instance, and probably many others, one of the courses had 8 students and the other had 10. Practically speaking, the two courses should have been combined into one of 18 students, but that would have required the professor to teach yet another course.

His seniority permitted him, unchecked, to split one course into two and thereby fulfil his entire fall obligation. From Fridays to Mondays, he had a four day break from campus obligations as was also the case

on Wednesdays. This was considered by the University
to be an entitlement for long service and tenure.

At another college, in a suburban location with a
history of strong and contentious faculty unionism, a
first-time study of student loads per faculty member
discovered that 65% of the full time faculty had annual
student loads of under 75 students, far short of the 120
minimum cited earlier in this chapter.

Further, well over 90% of all full time, tenured
faculty with annual salaries in excess of six figures had
annual student teaching loads of fewer than 60
students. There was only one tenured professor with an
annual teaching load in excess of the minimum 120. All
other faculty members with minimum, or more, student
loads were untenured junior faculty with, of course, the
lowest salaries. And, like the urban university
exemplar, the two highest paid faculty both had the
distinction of the two lowest student loads.

Given the inability to keep raising tuition rates,
prudent cost management is increasingly a necessity
that will likely impact long standing habits of spending
limited resources ineffectively. Such persistent habits
deny other expenditures that better serve students and
therefore retain more of them through to graduation.

An old adage declares that understanding the problem is half of the solution. Perhaps sharing such underperforming outcomes will prevent them from continuing. When that suburban, historically-unionized faculty cited above was presented with the student load data, the reaction was dominantly defensive and eventually led to discussion among faculty that had the potential, it seemed, to improve inequities and underperformance over time.

Understandably, taking on this kind of sacred cow can be dangerous and is avoided by most academic executives. But, enrollment-revenue dependent colleges have to start biting the bullet and confronting costs that cannot be sustained even if such cuts are negatively received by those who are affected. At best, such changes can perhaps be grandfathered which will, at least, correct the problem in generations ahead.

Examples of runaway costs are not limited to faculty underperformance.

Another example of a costly undertaking in need of attention at many colleges is tuition remission for employees. Many institutions have gone so far as to provide tuition-free enrollment for the dependents of all employees with no limit on the number of dependents.

The rationale for this generosity is multi-faceted and includes a low cost way of recruiting personnel to positions that are not very well paid. That 'low cost' rationale is based on the myth that such tuition-free dependents are filling empty seats in the classroom.

To the contrary, many colleges have so many employee dependents enrolled that additional classes are necessary requiring additional faculty at additional cost that is not being funded.

Some parents have been known to take any available job at the college where their children are enrolled and, in doing so, may be earning six-figure-equivalent salaries while two or three of their children enjoy a tuition-free college education. Then, those same parents resign upon the graduation of their children.

At the very least, colleges caught in this high cost program might consider a limit of one full time dependent at a time along with a qualifying number of years of employment. Perhaps something like a 25% remission after one year of employment, 50% after two years and 100% only after four years.

WINNERS
NEVER
QUIT

QUITTERS
NEVER
WIN

VINCE LOMBARDI

TOP PROBLEM #8

Trying to compete with Publics

The fact, cited many times throughout this book, that 80% of college students opt for the lower tuition of state universities and community colleges, is hard to disregard, even if you're a private, tuition-dependent college that cannot possibly compete with public institutions. That doesn't seem to stop far too many private colleges from trying. In doing so, as already outlined, such colleges are increasingly selling the product for less than it costs to make it, resulting in deficits that can lead, ultimately, to bankruptcy.

Not only are too many private colleges trying to compete with publics at a price level, they are also retooling their product to align with public institution academic programs.

Many public institutions, and especially community colleges, heavily focus on occupational training programs. Such academic majors tend to resonate strongly with today's college-bound families because of economic times that have fueled employment opportunity fears.

Thanks in large part to media alarmists, the value and cost of a college degree has come into doubt among large sectors of the college-bound population. College is wrongly no longer perceived, by many, as a prerequisite nor as a path to career and financial success. And, college costs are concurrently perceived as excessive, as outlined earlier, causing fear among the majority of college families that there exists a great likelihood that a college education will lead to heavy debt combined with unemployment.

To the contrary, college graduates continue to do much better, outpacing those without college degrees by about $20,000 a year while incurring, on average, about $30,000 in student loan debt. With that level of salary improvement, the debt can be paid off within a manageable range of time.

But perceptions are what they are and many private colleges are lining themselves up with public ones emphasizing occupational college degrees. While this may work, in part, for some private colleges located long distances from community colleges and state universities, those closer to public higher education are likely to back themselves into a financially unsustainable corner by trying to compete in this market.

The reality is that public institutions can provide what most employers will consider to be comparable programs.

And, they can do it for a fraction of the tuition cost that private colleges must charge, including those private colleges discounting in the 70% range.

While easier said than done, **perhaps the best strategy for private colleges is to stand tall and firm about what a college education should be, which is not, for most, to be a purveyor of specific occupational training.**

As all senior educators know, the majority of college-bound students have no idea what they really want to do for the rest of their lives and should be going to college to start discovering what that might be. In some cases, if not many, that decision may not come until after graduation. What a college education has traditionally achieved is to prepare its students to excel in whatever it is they finally decide upon when they are ready to make that decision.

In the case of today's Millenial and Generation Z cohorts, many will face multiple career experiences within their lifetime because of the way in which everything is evolving at an increasingly rapid pace. For most, the best college education is not narrowly defined into one occupational theme. But, while we

110

know this, 80% of college-bound families don't seem to be buying it.

Today's ten best job prospects: according to CareerBuilder.com, are:

1.   Truck driver
2.   Nurse
3.   Software Developer
4.   Marketing Manager
5.   Medical and Health Services Manager
6.   Sales Manager
7.   Network Systems Administrator
8.   Web Developer
9.   Industrial Engineer
10.   Computer Systems Analyst

Job prospects can change over time and it is hard to predict which of the above jobs will remain in the top ten throughout a Millennial and Generation Z lifetime. For several decades, gambling casino jobs flourished in central New Jersey because of the Atlantic City boom. Many regional community and state colleges opened degree programs in casino management and couldn't handle the demand. Today, those jobs are gone and the value of a degree in casino management isn't worth very much.

Another set of rankings is offered by Glassdoor, which compiles the median base salary of college academic majors. The top ranked majors are:

1.	Computer Science	$70,000
2.	Electrical Engineering	$68,400
3.	Mechanical Engineering	$68,000
4.	Chemical Engineering	$65,000
5.	Industrial Engineering	$64,400
6.	Info Technology	$64,000
7.	Civil Engineering	$61,500
8.	Statistics	$60,000
9.	Nursing	$58,900
10.	Mgmt Info Systems	$58,000
11.	Finance	$54,900
12.	Mathematics	$54,000
13.	Biomed Engineering	$52,800
14.	Accounting	$52,000
15.	Economics	$52,000
16.	Physics	$50,000
17.	Biotechnology	$50,000
18.	Architecture	$50,000
19.	Fashion Design	$50,000
20.	Business	$47,800
21.	Int'l Relations	$45,900
22.	Graphic Design	$45,800
23.	Marketing	$45,500
24.	English	$45,000
25.	Political Science	$45,000
26.	History	$45,000

What is illuminating about Glassdoor's listings is the number of 'non-occupational' majors, including English and History, that appear among the top paying, beyond entry level.

But, while college educators may know all this, too many of them acquiesce to what they perceive to be consumer demand and, in doing so, proceed to retool their institutions heavily toward narrowly-defined occupational majors. More often than not, those kinds of majors are offered in public institutions for a fraction of the cost, making for a hard sell that is bound to be financially unsustainable.

Not all college-bound families place job training and low cost as their driving influences in college choice. College-educated parents who are financially successful continue to enroll their students in private colleges that emphasize a broad-based college education over preparation for a specific job upon graduation. As a result, the marque private colleges and universities, regardless of their high costs, continue to be full to capacity and beyond.

Those private colleges struggling with enrollment and finances are perhaps better advised to look to those private colleges doing well, instead of public universities and community colleges. While the latter have most of the students, they also have massive amounts of government funding that private colleges are without and will not likely realize in the foreseeable future, if ever.

Admittedly, there are probably more private colleges today than there are students with financial wherewithal to pay private college tuition. Thus, it seems almost certain than some private colleges will close. Some are already closing. This trend seems certain to continue.

The colleges next to fail are those lacking the qualities sought by those who have the wherewithal to pay for college.

Emulating the public institutions, particularly in academic offerings and occupational majors, is almost definitely going to adversely influence the paying customers in search of the best college to which they can get their son or daughter admitted. In doing so, needed enrollment revenue is lost in exchange for students paying too little to cover the costs of financing the college.

COLLEGE DOES MORE
THAN PREPARE YOU
FOR YOUR FIRST JOB.

IT HELPS YOU
ANTICIPATE,
AND PERHAPS
EVEN CREATE,
YOUR FOURTH OR
FIFTH JOB
OR JOBS THAT
MAY NOT EVEN
YET EXIST.

DREW FAUST
PRESIDENT, HARVARD UNIVERSITY

TOP PROBLEM #9

Trying to do too many different things

I f private, enrollment-revenue-dependent colleges cannot compete with community colleges and state universities at a tuition-rate level, which they most certainly cannot, and if they also cannot offer the qualities that the college-educated and affluent families want for their college-bound children, what, then, is left to do?

First, no one strategic and programmatic direction fits all institutions. What has worked for one institution may fail horribly elsewhere.

Additionally, some strategic initiatives mix badly with others. No one institution can be all things to all people. For example, adult continuing education programs, particularly those with vocational occupational tracks, can mix badly with full time, undergraduate programs at a residential college.

An important consideration affecting feasibility of program initiatives is location. Private colleges and universities located in densely populated geographic centers have many options that remote, rural colleges are without.

Adult and continuing education, advanced certificate and mid-career, part-time graduate degree programs are among expansion opportunities that can be a meaningful financial revenue solution for urban centered private colleges. On-site corporate training programs have also been a financial savior for even

smaller private colleges in densely populated locales
where large corporate centers exist.

More remotely located colleges aren't likely to
find those kinds of markets within their neighborhoods,
especially if a community college or state university is
nearby. Rural public institutions are almost certain to
be serving what little of a market exists for continuing
and adult education, leaving the private college without
the ability to compete financially.

Those private colleges that 'own' their geographic
region with little to no public higher education presence
nearby can probably build alternative academic
programs for what limited market of adult and
professional demand might exist.

**However, private residential colleges
trying to hang onto their traditional
undergraduate enrollments have to take care
to preserve the status and stature of their
degrees.**

Offering part-time adult education programs can
reduce the perceived exclusivity of the college
experience which, in turn, can deter full-time 'paying

customers.' This is especially true if lower tuition rates are offered to part time students, many of whom end up enrolled in the same courses.

Any college aspiring to maintain, or achieve, stature as a venue for full-time residential undergraduate college students, most of whom can afford at least half of the tuition being charged, has to be careful not to 'water down the whiskey' by offering lower cost part-time programs. In time, this will 'water down' the core enrollment and worsen an already challenging situation.

College leaders also have to carefully weigh new ventures that are narrowly targeted, especially if they are directed toward what could be a short-lived trend. There probably isn't a college president alive who hasn't heard from a Trustee, a faculty member or someone in the admissions office that the College should launch a new major because of the student demand they are perceiving.

Many colleges have routinely responded to such perceived trends launching degrees in seemingly 'hot' professions like video games. Some decades ago, when Atlantic City was experiencing its emergence as the gambling center of the East, many adjacent colleges

introduced degree programs in casino management.
The graduates of these programs, now in their 40s or
50s, are finding their narrowly defined degrees working
against them as they face having to retool themselves
in light of the massive number of casino closures on the
Jersey shore.

As Alvin Toffler warned in his book Future
Shock, change is occurring at an increasingly fast pace.
How long video gaming, as a college degree, will likely
be of value is questionable. A couple of decades ago,
video tape stores, like Blockbuster, were as ubiquitous
as Starbucks coffee shops and there seemed no possible
end to their popularity. Now, they don't exist.

Similarly, owning photo processing shops seemed
like a service that consumers would always seek. After
all, when would people stop taking pictures, the film of
which had to be processed and the pictures which had to
be printed. Then, along came the iPhone.

The pace of change is making it that much more
compelling that a college education should be one that
prepares its graduates for change. The ability to adapt
to that change is probably the most important skill that
a college can give its students. And that is where a
classic college education wins the day as has

consistently been born out in the long term outcomes and successes of college graduates.

Colleges also have to take care in launching new programs. Over the past decade or so, on-line education has been perceived as a silver bullet for just about every college needing more enrollment revenue. However, launching such programs can be very costly and require skills that existing faculty in many colleges lack.

In the short run, stressed colleges already operating on fiscal fumes will be hard pressed to underwrite expensive new ventures unless they close down underperforming ones. Such closures invariably require the termination of tenured faculty, an action neither easy nor inexpensive.

What a college has to understand is that it cannot jump into every new venture touted in the media, or at professional association conferences, as having worked somewhere for some other college. Focusing on doing fewer things exceptionally well may be a better long term strategy.

THE DIRECTION
IN WHICH
YOUR EDUCATION
STARTS
WILL DETERMINE
YOUR FUTURE

PLATO

TOP PROBLEM #10

Employer needs
vs.
Student skills

A daunting dilemma for enrollment-revenue-dependent colleges is the chasm between what most Millennials and Generation Zs today are interested in doing vs. what most employers need in their new hires.

How do colleges reconcile needing to offer programs that prospective students will be drawn to while also providing training in the skills most needed by those students to obtain the best jobs?

In almost all surveys, STEM skills are at the top of the "most valuable" skill lists, namely:

Science

Technology

Engineering

Mathematics

STEM subject knowledge is a pre-requisite for health-related careers, computer technology and commerce as affirmed by the payscale.com list of top starting salaries by field of study:

Engineering	$65,000
Computer Science	$63,000
Management Info Systems	$57,000
Physics	$56,000
Applied Mathematics	$56,000
Economics	$52,000
Finance	$52,000
Government & Politics	$43,000
Construction Mgmt	$51,000
Bio-Sciences	$44,000

Notably, almost all the top paying jobs are in fields that require aptitude in math and science. Alarmingly, American students are weak in both areas.

In recent decades, American high school students have fallen off the global charts with respect to skills in science, math and, even, reading.

Both the National Center for Educational Statistics (NCES) and the International Organization for Economic Cooperation and Development (OECD) now rank American teenagers as 'below average' in all three categories but most chronically below in math and sciences.

The top of the list is dominated by Asian countries led by China, Singapore and Japan. In math, the United States actually ranks almost at the bottom of the 34 countries ranked.

In science, United States teenagers rank in the bottom seven. In reading, United States teenagers rank 22nd out of the 34 countries ranked.

The successful private colleges of the future will be those that have tooled themselves in ways that contribute meaningfully to the solution of this problem.

MATHEMATICS MEAN SCORE RANK

China	613	Slovenia	501
Singapore	573	Denmark	500
Hong Kong	561	New Zealand	500
Taiwan	560	Czech Republic	499
Korea	554	France	495
Liechtenstein	535	***OECD Average 494***	
Macao	538	United Kingdom	494
Japan	536	Iceland	493
Switzerland	531	Ireland	493
Netherlands	523	Luxembourg	490
Estonia	521	Norway	489
Finland	519	Portugal	487
Poland	518	Italy	485
Canada	518	Slovak Republic	482
Belgium	515	**USA**	**481**
Germany	514	Hungary	477
Vietnam	511	Israel	466
Austria	506		
Australia	504		

SCIENCE MEAN SCORE RANK

China	580	New Zealand	516
Hong Kong	555	Switzerland	515
Singapore	551	United Kingdom	514
Japan	547	Slovenia	514
Finland	545	Czech Republic	508
Estonia	541	Austria	506
Korea	538	Belgium	505
Vietnam	528	***OECD Average 501***	
Poland	526	France	499
Canada	525	Denmark	498
Liechtenstein	525	**USA**	**497**
Germany	524	Norway	495
Taiwan	523	Italy	494
Netherlands	522	Hungary	494
Ireland	522	Luxembourg	491
Macao	521	Iceland	478
Australia	521		

126

That said, what kind of 're-tooling' is possible that can reasonably resolve this problem? The circumstances over which colleges have little control is the curriculum in the elementary and high schools of America which are not successfully cultivating skills in math and science. This problem was identified decades ago by The Carnegie Commission's "A Nation at Risk" which, among other influences, noted that anyone with math and science aptitude could earn a much higher salary outside of teaching. That problem persists to this day without having been resolved and has thereby placed American aptitude in these important skills in the lowest positions in global ranking.

The higher education community has not really contributed to the solution and has, in many ways, moved away from it. Perhaps colleges should consider reintroducing courses like basic algebra, chemistry and physics into the core college curriculum in an attempt to develop these skills that weren't successfully inculcated in high school. To do so, colleges might also have to pay such math and science faculty a premium in order to lure them away from the private sector.

In doing so successfully, they will be graduating students who are in strong demand for top paying careers, and hopefully drawing more students to enroll because of that outcome.

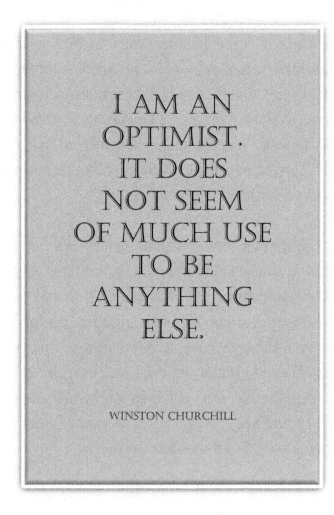

I AM AN OPTIMIST. IT DOES NOT SEEM OF MUCH USE TO BE ANYTHING ELSE.

WINSTON CHURCHILL

NORMAN R. SMITH

TOP PROBLEM #11

Making the case
for
Liberal Arts

While all college educators realize the essential role that a broad-based liberal arts education represents in lifetime personal and professional success, the sad reality today is that the majority of college-bound families don't buy into it.

Liberals Arts is too often characterized as a near certain guarantee of unemployment after graduation.

Failing to find applicants for classic liberal arts undergraduate education, colleges struggling to maintain enrollments have been acquiescing to consumer demand, understandably, and retooling to offer academic programs with explicit occupational outcomes. The problem with this, as already covered earlier in this book, is that less-expensive community colleges and state universities can offer those same programs at a much lower cost making it very difficult for enrollment-revenue-dependent colleges to successfully compete at a financially sustainable level.

Perhaps a more viable solution for private colleges is to 're-package' liberal arts and go back to the basics of a classic college education that has sustained the American higher educational system as one of the few US products that is viewed globally as top shelf. And, speaking of top shelf and contrary to public perception, **a significant cohort of America's most successful people did not major in occupationally-themed academic programs as undergraduates.**

Notable are corporate CEOs. More often than not, the presidents of America's largest businesses did not major in business as undergraduates. Perhaps many more of them went on to earn MBA's after their basic college education, but their undergraduate focus was broad-based in studies that have traditionally been referred to as the liberal arts. More often than not, these remarkably successful people, including international leaders, affirm that non-occupational undergraduate education served them well.

Undergraduate Majors
of
Top Corporate CEOs

Campbell Soup	Denise Morrison	Economics & Psych
United-Continental	Jeff Smisek	Economics
Host Hotels	Edward Walter	Political Science
Overstock.com	Patrick Byrne	Chinese Studies
Sears Holdings	Edward Lampert	Economics
FEDEX	Fred Smith	Economics
Time Warner	Robert Marcus	Political Science
21st Century FOX	James Murdoch	History
Best Buy	Bradbury Anderson	Sociology
American Int'l	Peter Hancock	Philosophy Economics
Goldman Sachs	Lloyd Blankfein	History
Starbucks	Howard Schultz	Communications
Merck & Co	Kenneth Frazier	Political Science
Citigroup	Michael Corbat	Economics
Bank of America	Brian Moynihan	History
YouTube	Susan Wojcicki	History & Literature
Whole Foods	John Mackey	Philosophy & Religion
Avon	Andrea Jones	English
Hewlett Packard	Carly Fiorina	History & Philosophy
HBO	Richard Plepler	Government
PayPal	Peter Thiel	Philosophy
Ted Turner	Turner Broadcasting	Classics

Undergraduate Majors
Of Government Leaders

United Nations Ambassador Susan Rice	History
California Governor Jerry Brown	Classics
Former Vice President Joe Biden	History
Former Secretary/Senator Hillary Clinton	Political Science
UK Prime Minister Theresa May	Geography
Germany Chancellor Angela Merkel	Chemistry
Supreme Court Chief Justice John Roberts	History
Speaker of the House Paul Ryan	Economics
Former Secretary of State John Kerry	Political Science

According to payscale.com, **employers today are reporting that most of their college graduate hires are chronically deficient in the skills they most need to climb career ladders.**

The top ten skills, in rank order by frequency of response, that employers most frequently cited as lacking or missing altogether are:

Critical Thinking/Problem Solving	60%
Attention to detail	56%
Communication	48%
Ownership	44%
Leadership	44%
Writing Proficiency	44%
Public Speaking	39%
Teamwork Skills	36%
Data Analysis	36%
Industry Specific Software	34%

All of these skills, as any college educator knows, are qualities developed in undergraduate academic programs that are broad-based.

While it goes against the tenets of conventional wisdom, at least in the minds of college-bound families, **the value of a college education is best characterized as preparation to become a leader in whatever it is each student finally discovers as their lifetime purpose.**

"Liberal Arts" is widely misunderstood to represent a political ideology rather than the concept of being liberally educated. That leftist political ideology is combined with the view that arts means painting, singing and acting. Put all that together and it has become a 'product' that too many parents won't consider.

The Council of Independent Colleges has been working fervently to change that perception and to instead remind everyone that 'liberal arts' is the foundation of America's great higher education tradition. Their efforts toward that end continue to be a slow, steep uphill undertaking.

Because of the typical negative reaction to liberal arts, perhaps colleges should try other terminology like core curriculum, or across-the-curriculum learning, in order to make the case for aspiring to be a broadly and comprehensively learned person. It is that kind of college graduate who will have built the strongest foundation to be a leader in whatever field ultimately is chosen. And it is that kind of college graduate who is best prepared to adapt to the changes that will confront Millennials, and the emerging Generation Z, throughout their lifetimes.

To this end, a number of colleges and universities are introducing the concept of leadership training as an alternative characterization of broad-based liberal arts. Widener University in Pennsylvania has received some very favorable media accounts for their Oskin Leadership Institute which provides a core of leadership courses increasingly required of all Widener undergraduates.

Leadership skills are learned. Many of the college courses least associated with specific job training are among those fundamental to leadership training.

Along with leadership skills, many contend that today's Millennial and Generation Zs must be adept in:

Technology
Globalization
Commerce

Millennials and Generation Zs 'literate' in these three fields are going to be most in demand and will be the leaders of their generation.

Recognize though, that these three forces are not primary undergraduate majors. Rather, they are areas of competence that are realized through knowledge that is accumulated via an array of courses and disciplines.

Some might say multi-disciplinary or across the curriculum because, for instance, globalization means a world perspective competency that can include macroeconomics, languages, world history, global politics, multi-national commerce, and, of course, travel. To that end, all colleges should be exploring ways to retool that insure their undergraduate program heavily responds to inculcating world awareness throughout their curriculum. Included is the example that institutions like Goucher College have already set; namely, requiring that all undergraduates study a semester abroad as a requirement for graduation.

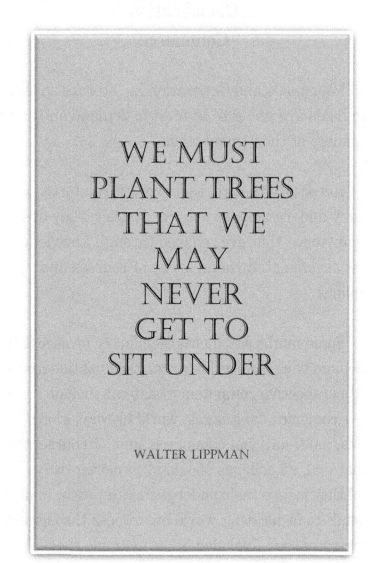

WE MUST
PLANT TREES
THAT WE
MAY
NEVER
GET TO
SIT UNDER

WALTER LIPPMAN

TOP PROBLEM #12

Debt

The Garden of Eden had its forbidden fruit which, for private enrollment-dependent colleges today, can be justly compared to incurring major debt. While the prospect of borrowed millions may be very tempting, the consequences can be deadly, and have been for some colleges already.

In principle, there is nothing wrong with incurring debt if the money is used in ways that will generate additional revenue. Businesses routinely borrow money in order to prosper.

However, today's Internet information age, combined with a media propensity to scrutinize private college costs, have put colleges under a microscope whereby 'being in debt' is often construed as being in financial trouble. When the latter characterization comes to the attention of prospective students and their parents, heavy institutional indebtedness can close the door on enrollment prospects.

Colleges today have to be very wary about their level of debt. The rule of thumb varies. NACUBO has at times set the debt limit for colleges in the range of one-third to one-half of net annual operating revenues. Net revenues are the bottom line after tuition-discounting has been deducted.

So, if the college's net revenues after discounting are $50 million, their debt being serviced should not exceed $25 million and should probably be under $20 million.

Many colleges have precariously incurred debts well over 100% of their net annual operating revenues as lenders have seemingly not been deterred by NACUBO guidelines. This is probably because the borrowing college lays out revenue projections that are too often inflated dreams hopefully to be realized as a result of the way in which the borrowed money will be spent. Yet "spend it and they will come" often doesn't turn out that way.

As any business will affirm, 'you have to spend money to make money.' Colleges seeking to borrow funds to build new facilities, like student housing, typically declare that the borrowed money will increase enrollments and thereby inflate the net revenue levels. Creditors buy into that rationale and the college ends up heavily in debt with even greater expectations placed upon its future outcomes by creditors.

As long as the indebted college delivers on revenue growth promises, the debt incurred probably won't adversely affect anything. But, if the projected growth doesn't fulfil, or even exceed, debtor and debt rating agency expectations, the college faces being pummeled with adverse publicity that has prospective students and their families crossing the college off their list.

This adverse publicity can arise even if the indebted college is paying its debt servicing consistently on time.

Creditors, debt raters, accreditors and government overseers have all gotten into the act of scrutinizing the financial health of indebted colleges according to their 'dash board' criteria.

Each such evaluator posts their opinions on their respective websites which are readily accessible to high school college counselors, parents and prospective students themselves, not to mention the media. *The Chronicle of Higher Education*, for one, routinely runs stories about colleges that have had their debt 'downgraded' by rating agencies like Standard & Poor's and Moody's. Accreditors are increasingly posting their evaluations of financial health next to the accreditation status of their member institutions.

These downgrades have an alarming effect on prospective customers, even, as noted above, when the indebted college has been paying its debt on time. The ratings are based on prospects that the debt may not continue to be honored. Those prospects are derived from assessments of financial liquidity that, in the evaluator's opinion, isn't rich enough for long term security.

As a result, these gloom-and-doom forecasts become a self-fulfilling prophecy because they contribute to the decline of the indebted college's enrollment revenues.

A particularly extreme exemplar can now be recounted and maybe heeded; namely, Dowling College on Long Island which closed down in 2016 after a number of years of crippling enrollment decline.

Dowling was the victim of two principal mistakes that could happen at many colleges.

Debt was one of them and perhaps the straw that broke the camel's back.

A little background: Dowling College was spun off from Adelphi University in the late 1960s. Its main campus was the centerpiece of the William Vanderbilt estate on the south shore of Long Island between the Hamptons and JFK International Airport. Its main building was the grand Vanderbilt Mansion on a striking water inlet leading to the south shore Atlantic.

For decades, Dowling flourished in the high density population of Long Island and was a key 'feeder' of school teachers for the myriad school systems of Nassau and Suffolk counties. Eight school superintendents were Dowling College alumni and enthusiastic employers of new College graduates. Dowling couldn't graduate enough teachers to keep up with demand. Especially lucrative was their evening and weekend master's programs for working school teachers, all of whom were required by the State to earn a graduate degree within about five years of having earned their undergraduate degrees.

With nearly 6,000 students, Dowling College flourished with more money than needed, especially because of the high 'net revenue' margin master's program for teachers.

This prosperity brought about visions of future grandeur that, in the 1990s, resulted in their acquiring a 100-acre plot of land adjacent to Brookhaven Airport, about 25 miles east of their Vanderbilt campus. The plan was to build an aviation school that would be a national leader in the field.

As the land was undeveloped, the College borrowed $75 million by issuing bonds that were publicly traded and therefore subject to being rated, by Standard & Poor's, and the like, according to their assessment of the debtor's creditworthiness.

Dowling then spent all those millions on an impressive renovation of the 100 acres that, in addition to an aviation center and a hotel-like student residence, included a collection of outdoor playing fields, all with the best artificial turf available, not to mention stadium seats and night lighting. As for the aviation program, a collection of airplanes was purchased so that aviation majors could learn to fly. This impressive new campus was opened by Astronaut Neil Armstrong. The sky was the proverbial limit.

This massive investment resulted in fewer than 200 aviation majors, hardly enough to cover the instructional costs, not to mention the debt incurred. That apparently didn't matter, though, because the 6,000 other students, and especially the 1,400 teachers earning their master's degrees, gave the College more than enough revenue to cover the stand-alone losses at the Brookhaven campus.

Until, that is, the new Millennium changed the landscape for teaching jobs on Long Island. Around 2007, jobs in teaching started to disappear along with state funding for basic education.

As Dowling had most of its 'eggs' in the education program baskets, enrollments in all their core programs crashed. Between 2009 and 2013, total enrollments dropped from 6,000 to 2,600 students. The 'cash cow' master's program was particularly hard hit with 1,000 of the over 1,300 students disappearing. After all, if no new teachers were being hired, there were no teachers who needed to earn their master's degrees.

While this enrollment decline was massive and resulted in major rounds of personnel terminations, particularly in the education program areas, the College continued to enroll nearly 3,000 students which should have been enough for them to re-tool and continue to exist.

That would have been possible had it not been for the debt.

The $50+ million in outstanding public bond debt was now in excess of 100% of net operating revenues. Standard & Poor's, along with other bond rating agencies, were quick to condemn the debt and thereby downgrade the creditworthiness of Dowling College.

Accreditors also challenged the debt and highlighted that impediment even though evaluation teams appointed by the accreditors applauded and commended the quality of the faculty, and the management and the student body. Despite this, they declared that Dowling was 'in jeopardy' of losing accreditation because of the financial problems caused by declines in education enrollments combined with burdensome debt.

In reaction, the media headlined the 'financial crisis' and 'accreditation jeopardy' at Dowling College implying its likely demise. That was all high school college counselors, along with prospective students and their parents, needed to hear.

Almost immediately thereafter, applications started to disappear and currently enrolled students started to transfer elsewhere. All this made the servicing of debt impossible to the point where, only five years later, Dowling was defeated and had to close.

Dowling could not have been in a more populous applicant market. It had a beautiful campus. Its most recent accreditation had applauded the quality of the faculty and student experience.

Three caveats to learn from Dowling's death are:

Don't put all your eggs in one basket. Dowling's heavy dependence on teacher jobs was crippling.

Don't borrow money that is subject to public credit ratings from agencies like Standard & Poor's and Moody's.

Their ratings, often based on long term fiscal health predictions, are widely published and can scare away the customers.

While it may be necessary to spend money to make money, don't assume that all spending in all areas will succeed.

Most importantly (caveat three): Don't borrow money that can only be paid back if

**success is realized from ambitious and
expensive undertakings.**

Maybe businesses can declare bankruptcy,
reorganize and move on.

Colleges cannot do the same if they want to stay
in business. Once a private college is known to be in
financial crisis that forces a bankruptcy filing, any hope
of recruiting and enrolling paying students is over.

When an enrollment-revenue-dependent college
loses the confidence of the college-bound public, it bids
farewell to its very existence.

For those colleges already heavily in debt and
increasingly unable to make payments because of
revenue declines, the prospects for solutions aren't
attractive, but aren't impossible. In recent years, some
severely distressed institutions have managed to relieve
themselves of significant debt by calling upon creditors
to take what is colloquially referred to as a 'hair cut.'

Getting such creditors to write off debt is not a
panacea and can be accompanied by outcomes that can
be tortuous, hazardous and even fatal. Institutions

seeking debt forgiveness will likely face a series of traumatic episodes that can include forbearance agreements, litigation, bankruptcies, and, most devastating in many cases, media exposure.

With the advent of the Internet, news never goes away as was once the case with yesterday's newspaper. And, small town newspapers read by a very limited audience now routinely post their stories thereby making them available to everyone everywhere.

Dowling College should serve as a dire warning that major debt is an undertaking that all enrollment-revenue dependent colleges should avoid. Never mind that borrowing is a routine business practice deemed necessary for realizing additional income. While the same practice should logically apply to enrollment-revenue colleges, the consequences of failure are too risky and potentially fatal.

With the volatility of applicant pools for private higher education, the risk of incurring excessive debt is too precarious to undertake any more. While the numbers vary among experts, NACUBO has cited the absolute debt ceiling for any college as not exceeding 30% of annual

net revenues. That is probably as good a rule of thumb
as any that exists.

LIVE WITHIN
YOUR MEANS
&
NEVER
BE IN DEBT

ANDREW JACKSON

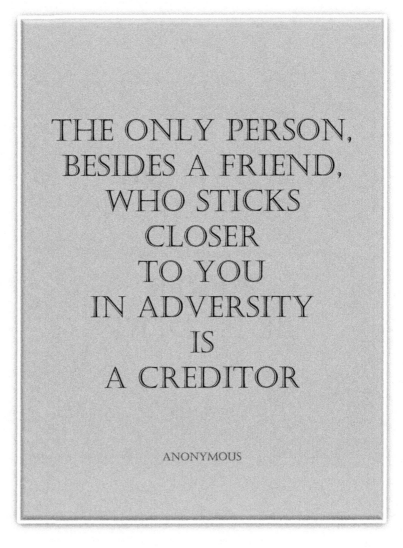

THE ONLY PERSON,
BESIDES A FRIEND,
WHO STICKS
CLOSER
TO YOU
IN ADVERSITY
IS
A CREDITOR

ANONYMOUS

TOP PROBLEM #13

Fund Raising

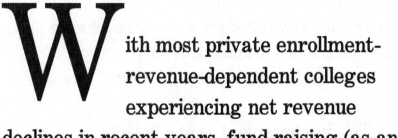**W**ith most private enrollment-
revenue-dependent colleges
experiencing net revenue
declines in recent years, fund raising (as an
alternative source of revenue) has too often
been perceived as a panacea comparable to
winning the Powerball lottery. While

fundraising shouldn't be dismissed, it also shouldn't be viewed as a silver bullet that can satisfactorily replace significant reductions in traditional net enrollment revenue. Thus, college presidents called upon to spend half of their time on the road in search of donations may not be making the most prudent use of their time and energies.

There is no single formula for how presidential time should be spent and how much of that time should be dedicated to any specific facet of the college's operations. That division of labor is greatly dependent on where the college finds itself in its individual hierarchy of needs.

Any college fortunate enough to be fully enrolled and annually flooded with applications from students whose families can afford private college tuition is likely to be in the position to apportion a large amount of presidential attention to traveling and fund raising.

The inconvenient truth is that traditional colleges must come to grips with the historic core mission, their traditional undergraduate operations, and resolve

whatever it is that is impeding outcomes that secure enrollment revenue. Until resolved, this is where the President's efforts should be heavily focused.

Most enrollment-revenue-dependent colleges, which is the overwhelming majority of private colleges throughout the US, are 90%, or more, dependent on student tuition payments.

A small college, say, with about 1,500 under-graduates and charging $35,000 tuition is realizing $26 million annually if discounting that tuition rate at 50%. Fundraising to realize an endowment of $500 million would be necessary to obtain that same kind of annual revenue.

So, college presidents spending half time on fund raising, if any really do, are spending too much of their time on an effort that is very unlikely to result in anything close to the annual revenues needed by the college.

Of the approximately 2,000 private colleges and universities in America, only 175 or so (less than 10%) have endowments of $500 million or more. All but several dozen of those 175 are large universities; Harvard, Yale and Princeton among the most heavily endowed, as noted above.

Most of the several dozen smaller colleges with $500 million or more endowments are venerable institutions like Swarthmore, Amherst, Vassar and Wellesley Colleges.

Presidents and Trustees should focus their efforts on the cultivation of major donors, leaving most of all other giving, like alumni annual giving, to staff. However, major donors should not be delegated to staff for cultivation. The president and the Board of Trustees have to make major donor prospects their personal project.

Today, the two most important members of a college fund raising team are the major gifts officer and the planned giving officer.

More often than not, the most successful major gifts officer is someone who can relate effectively to donor prospects who are 70 and older. Such prospects, presumably wealthy, are at that time in their lives when they know they have enough wealth to live comfortably for the rest of their lives, have set aside additional money for their children and their children's children, and still have additional money to leave a legacy of importance to them.

An exemplary major gifts officer (who at a small college should probably always be the Vice President for Advancement) was David Long at Skidmore College. Long partnered with Skidmore President Joseph Palamountain during the 1970s and 80s when Skidmore decided to relocate its campus and build an entirely new College on the opposite side of Saratoga Springs, New York.

David Long's persona was that of a senior statesman who could readily pass as a college president, making him a perfect complement to Palamountain who also conveyed the presidential gravitas and charm that is key to successful major donor cultivation.

Together, David Long and Joe Palamountain had a long run of successful major donor outcomes that built the new campus and laid a foundation for Skidmore's success to this day. Upon Palamountain's death in the late 1980s, Long repeated his success at Wagner

College on Staten Island by locating major donor opportunities that resulted in the most successful fund raising years in Wagner's history.

David Long was the essential door opener in both cases, but presidential and Board involvement in the cultivation of those opened doors was as essential. Without someone like David Long, though, those doors are too often never found in the first place.

An equally valuable fund raising executive in more recent times has become the planned giving officer. The best models have often proven to be people who don't necessarily present themselves as fund raisers, but rather as financial planning counselors; because that is what they are.

With almost non-existent interest rates on savings this past decade, retirees are finding it difficult to identify low-risk places for their wealth that generate reasonable levels of income off which they can then live comfortably.

In response, many colleges and universities have created a financial planning advising office, working out of the development operation, that offers free counsel toward structuring a way in which the 'donor' can have

an optimum revenue stream better than that which
might conventionally be available through conservative
investments like bank certificates of deposit, while at
the same time providing the College with a legacy trust.

The monies ultimately realized by the college
from these longer-term financial arrangements may be
decades away, but can be built into what eventually
could represent major windfalls for the college. Such
constructs are typically irrevocable and can therefore
become reliable future assets that can eventually give
the college a substantial endowment.

While both major gifts and planned giving are
sources of significant revenues for a college, they don't
replace the amount of time that the president and the
college itself must spend, first and foremost, on
realizing satisfactory levels of enrollment income.

**Colleges should also carefully scrutinize
the total costs being incurred to raise funds.**
In an effort to optimize the chances of winning the
Powerball, some colleges are spending too much money
on buying lottery tickets.

One large, urban university was unknowingly annually spending $1 million <u>more</u> on fund raising staff and operations than it was realizing in annual gifts. Another smaller college was found to be spending everything it received in annual giving on staff and operating costs. In both cases, it was even worse than that, as a large portion of the annual giving total included Trustee gifts that would likely have been realized, through Presidential and Board Chair efforts, even if there hadn't been a development staff in place.

No college should spend more than 25% of what it receives in gifts, on the expenses associated with getting those gifts.

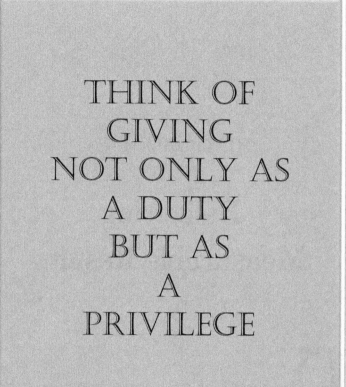

THINK OF
GIVING
NOT ONLY AS
A DUTY
BUT AS
A
PRIVILEGE

JOHN D. ROCKEFELLER

TOP PROBLEM #14

Delivering
Measurable Results

The value of a college degree, when measured against the cost of getting it, has come into question in recent years, as observed throughout this book. Among the reasons for such doubt is how difficult it seems to be, nowadays, for college graduates to obtain gainful employment. Some reports have cited as many as half of all college graduates being either unemployed or working at a job not really requiring the college education they had just earned. A particularly sobering report, not so long ago, declared that as many as a third of all college graduates under 30 years of age were continuing to live at home because they were unable to obtain a job paying enough to enable them to enjoy a standard of living comparable to the life they enjoyed with their parents.

Times have changed for Millennials and Generation Zs. Back in the 1960s and 70s, most college seniors could rely upon prospective employers appearing on campus and conducting job interviews that somehow seemed to place all graduates into full-time paying jobs shortly after Commencement (with the exception of those going on to graduate school, who, of course, were similarly moving on to higher plateaus.)

Today, those senior year corporate recruiters are few and far between, largely being only in those few occupational fields experiencing high demand including computer technology and health services (e.g., nursing, radiology, etc.).

Also, many employers are taking too much advantage of internship status, instead of offering full-time jobs. Thus, college graduates are subjected to temporary, low paying internship assignments even after graduating, which provide no benefits and uncertain prospects for full time jobs.

Even President Barak Obama questioned the advisability of a college education that wasn't directly linked to specific occupational preparation. At the same time, it remains a reality that most high school seniors have no idea what they want to do for the rest of their lives when entering college, and realistically shouldn't as upwards of **75% of all college students change their major while in college.**

Most colleges have not adequately adapted to the way in which opportunities after graduation are now realized. Preparing for the next chapter after graduation today has become a four-year undertaking in which the colleges themselves need to be more actively engaged.

Students today cannot assume that a college transcript and diploma, along with a resume, is all they need to become gainfully employed upon graduation.

They also have to be discovered which can take almost as much effort during their undergraduate years as the coursework.

Put bluntly, it is not just what you know (which is essential) but also who knows that you know what you know. Today's college graduate, in other words, has to get discovered by someone who can open doors that are otherwise closed.

There aren't enough jobs that need to be filled, but jobs often get created when prospective employers discover someone with whom they are impressed. Getting to that discoverer is the challenge. Helping students get discovered is, at many colleges, an essential service that is not as intensely part of the core undergraduate program as it probably should be.

Unfortunately, the typical college career development and placement office has not changed all that much since the 1960s and is usually minimally staffed with personnel who largely view themselves as counselors for those students who seek their advice and assistance in tasks like preparing a resume. Most such operations are part of the student services infrastructure and, in many cases, are minimally connected to the faculty and academic programs.

Some colleges have risen to the 'new norm' and taken it upon themselves to at least expose their students, while enrolled, to experientials in the 'outside' world. *US News & World Report* cited a group of colleges that went so far as to require such external experience as a condition for graduation. Those schools so cited included Wagner College, Elmira College and Bennington College.

Accreditors are also increasingly concerned about what they typically refer to as 'outcomes' which heavily focuses on what graduates do next and how that relates to what they studied while in college.

All this makes a compelling argument for colleges to retool their traditional career development and placement offices into an infrastructure that is more integral to the core activities of the college and, ideally, is charged with insuring that every full-time student has a relevant place to go after graduation. This will only be possible if the career development staff itself is larger and more professional and more integrated into the institution's academic programs.

Such an effort also has to be a more integral part of faculty responsibility and obligation, especially for those students aspiring to

attend graduate school upon completion of their undergraduate degrees. While some faculty advisors have always been proactive in helping insure the post-graduate success of their students, such a responsibility has rarely been a fundamental obligation for which the faculty member is held accountable.

Going forward, therefore, new infrastructures need to be developed that tie the faculty and the post-graduate (career development) functions together and perhaps under the same authority, namely, the Academic Affairs umbrella.

I have yet to come across an exemplar that can cite an outcome that accounts for each and every graduate. Few admissions recruiting programs include a publication that lists all graduates and where they went immediately after Commencement.

Any college that builds such a comprehensive program, in tandem with concurrent comprehensive successful outcomes, will possess a very powerful admissions recruitment lure that will almost certainly assure healthy enrollments.

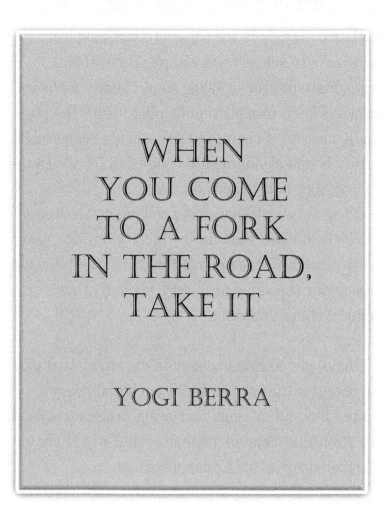

WHEN
YOU COME
TO A FORK
IN THE ROAD,
TAKE IT

YOGI BERRA

TOP PROBLEM #15

Litigation

NO list of *"Top Problems Facing Colleges"* today would be complete without noting the crippling effect of lawyers and regulatory organizations, including accreditors and government agencies. The combined effect of these two monsters is in the process of putting smaller colleges out of business and there appears little hope of the situation improving. In fact, there is every indication that the situation will worsen.

The problem isn't a new one. But like so many runaway trains, nothing has been done to prevent the problem from intensifying over the past several decades.

Over 25 years ago, in 1989, then Boston University President, John Silber, authored a book titled "Straight Shooting: What's Wrong with America and How to Fix It." A particularly haunting chapter was "The Litigious Society" which lamented **the excessive number of lawyers in America which Silber warned was rapidly creating 'a society overrun by hordes of lawyers, hungry as locusts.'**

At that time, Silber cited the existence of 650,000 lawyers making for, in 1989, one lawyer for every 365 Americans. . .one client per day for each lawyer. He warned that law schools were graduating lawyers at rates that far exceeded population growth. If both demographics continued at the 1989 rate, every man, woman and child in America would have to have a law degree in 2074, then 85 years away. By comparison,

Western European countries, 25 years ago, averaged 1500 citizens per lawyer, only 25% the relative density of lawyers as compared to the US.

Silber's ominous warning, decades later, seems on track.

Today, there are twice as many lawyers as in 1989. With over 1.3 million licensed lawyers, according to the American Bar Association, there is now one lawyer for every 245 Americans. And, they indeed seem to be proving themselves "as hungry as locusts."

Anyone with a television set has viewed commercials promising viewers the prospect of 'winning' millions of dollars by launching lawsuits that cost the client nothing unless "we win." Known as contingency fees, lawyers instead take a major percentage of the settlement paid by the person or institution being sued.

While colleges are not alone as the targets of these contingency lawsuits, they are among the institutions most financially damaged as most colleges are without deep pockets to pay for million-dollar settlements.

With so many 'hungry' lawyers out there, the incidence of lawsuits aimed at colleges is growing at a crippling pace.

It is not uncommon nowadays for contingency lawyers to represent students who contend that they were adversely graded for any number of reasons that can include discrimination because of race, ethnicity, sex, etc.

Colleges are also lawsuit targets when students engage in hostility toward each other because these lawyers contend that the College should have been able to prevent whatever it was that caused the conflict. Moreover, any member of the College faculty or administration who says anything that is construed as offensive by a student can now anticipate the prospect of that student launching a lawsuit.

Even when these lawsuits have absolutely no merit, and, in the judgment of College legal counsel, can readily be won in court, the College is advised that the cost of winning the lawsuit (i.e., legal fees) will likely reach into six figures and that it will therefore be less expensive to settle out of court for a mere five figure amount. Many call this 'green-mail', arguably a fair-enough variation of blackmail.

A quarter of a century ago, Silber called upon the US government to adopt the British legal model whereby failed lawsuits, deemed by justices to have been frivolous, result in all court costs, and the legal costs of the defendant, being paid by those who brought the unwarranted lawsuit to court. Such a potential consequence greatly reduces the incidence of multi-million dollar greenmail suits.

Of course, such a provision would also put hundreds of thousands of lawyers out of business. So, forty years later, nothing has been done to change the American legal system which is increasingly crippling the financial wherewithal of many including small private colleges.

Why has nothing been done? Perhaps a major part of the reason is the number of lawyers who are law makers. While the numbers are declining, over half of the US Senators cite their profession as lawyers thereby giving them every incentive to enact laws that lawyers will then challenge or defend on behalf of their clients. After all, all these new lawyers being graduated by too many law schools need work to do.

To illustrate this, the Code of Federal Regulations, when it was first published in 1938 contained 18,000 pages. Three decades later, in 1970, there were 54,000 pages. In half that time, by 1984, there were 100,000 pages. During the Obama administration alone, an additional 600,000 pages were reportedly added (more the fault of Congress than the Obama administration).** While not every page represents a law (only about one-third of the contents are laws), it is nevertheless clear that more laws result in more litigation which results in more legal fees, thereby feeding the continued growth of the legal profession.

Thus, more laws and lawyers result in more money being spent by clients defending themselves and, in the case of colleges, less money available to teach students.

**Source: George Washington University Center for Regulatory Studies.

THE MINUTE
YOU READ
SOMETHING YOU
CAN'T
UNDERSTAND,

YOU CAN
ALMOST
BE SURE
THAT IT WAS
DRAWN UP BY
A LAWYER.

WILL ROGERS

TOP PROBLEM #16

Government & Accreditation Oversight

Boston University President John Silber also noted, in 1989, that the problem isn't limited to contingency personal injury lawyers. He further warned that government and compliance regulation was getting way out of hand forcing small private colleges to spend far too much money, most of which comes out of the pockets of students and families who cannot readily afford it.

In his book, Silber recounts a complaint filed by a faculty member with the Equal Employment Opportunity Commission of the US Government. Boston University challenged the complaint and prevailed in court. But it cost the University $500,000 in legal fees, none of which were reimbursed by the federal government. That was forty years ago. Over the past four decades, legal fees have consistently outpaced most other costs, including tuition.

Today, it is almost financially impossible for smaller, private colleges to legally defend themselves against government regulatory investigations and complaints.

Of particular consequence to colleges today is Title IX compliance. The US Department of Education's Office of Civil Rights has moved aggressively in recent years with respect to the role of the College in accusations filed by victims of date rape, to name just one criminal violation that has now become the responsibility of colleges to investigate and adjudicate. That a college, whose mission it is to teach, must now become a court of law places an enormous responsibility and burden on thousands of colleges with no infrastructure to conduct a criminal court of law case. But that is fundamentally what the federal government is expecting and demanding.

No matter how careful a college administration tries to be, it is not really qualified to undertake the prosecution and adjudication of a criminal offense. Moreover, no matter the decision that comes out of such a 'trial,' one side is going to be unhappy and will undoubtedly hire a personal injury contingency lawyer to sue the college for legal malpractice of one sort or another.

Additionally, the federal government itself reviews the way in which the college attempts to adjudicate the alleged felony. Should the college err in any way, the Office of Civil Rights places the college on its censure list which the college is required to publish on its website, thereby informing prospective students and their families that the college has violated federal compliance laws with respect to felony rape.

Such a federal government-mandated condemnation is almost certain to deter prospective students and their families from associating with the college, except perhaps if those families realize that the violating colleges and universities are growing in the hundreds and include some of America's most prestigious universities, including the Ivy League.

If major universities like Cornell, with generous infrastructures of full time legal counsel, are vulnerable to being judged out of compliance with their legal obligation to adjudicate criminal felonies like rape, smaller colleges are even less likely to have the legal infrastructure necessary to successfully comply.

Smaller private colleges can simply not afford to finance and staff courts of law mandated to conduct criminal investigations or to convene courts of law. Such criminal allegations should be referred to district attorneys and be handled the same way in which any other felony is processed. The college should have no role except to cooperate with the officials who are qualified to deal with such criminal allegations.

That said, colleges and universities should not be exempt from responsibility for doing everything they can to prevent such violations of the law, and to try to educate their students with regard to the seriousness of violating the law, and its consequences.

But, the federal government is impractically turning the prosecution and adjudication of a felony crime over to an institution of higher education. In doing so, as noted above, the government is almost certainly subjecting the college to civil lawsuits regardless of the outcome, and potentially burying the college in legal costs that can exhaust needed monies at a time when fiscal sustainability is already challenged.

If this were not enough straw to break many camels' backs, regional accreditors have also added burdens.

Accreditors, it would seem logical to presume, exist in order to assess whether students attending an educational institution are being educated in accordance with the claims laid out by the educational institution and also in compliance with fundamental standards of educational excellence. While that is very much a part of the accreditation process, accrediting organizations have expanded their oversight into a variety of related areas that include governance, management and financial health.

There exist, in most cases, over a dozen criteria with which a college must successfully be judged as being in compliance, in order to be accredited. Many of those criteria do focus on the quality of teaching and learning, as they should.

But today, it is no secret that many private colleges, especially smaller ones, are financially challenged and struggle to keep their financial heads above water.

If a college is deemed in compliance with its responsibility to teach students effectively, but is not in compliance with the standards set for financial optimum health, some accreditors will deem the college to be "IN JEOPARDY" of losing accreditation if the college doesn't satisfactorily improve its financial health according to the standards set by the accreditor.

As noted above, in some cases that ominous declaration of 'jeopardy' is published on the accreditor's website accessible to all and studied carefully by high school college counselors. When a school counselor sees "jeopardy," parents are invariably advised to consider other colleges. Many such colleges-in-jeopardy have been concurrently praised by the same accreditor for the commitment of their faculty and the productivity of students. But those latter commendations tend to go unnoticed when 'in jeopardy of losing accreditation' is in website headlines. Such prominence can also lead to media headlines, including those on Internet media websites.

Accreditors will justifiably and understandably defend their processes presumably because financially-challenged colleges should be known to the public as such fiscal shortages can, perhaps, adversely affect investment in teaching resources. While that may well be defensible, going so far as to publish the prospect of losing accreditation IF improvements are not made to finances attaches a massive ball and chain that deters college prospects which, in turn, results in major financial losses for the college. Which, in turn, prevents the college from making the very corrections for which they are being cited. *For the loss of a nail. . .*

This onus seems especially unfair on those colleges that are concurrently being lauded for the quality of their educational product. They are doing their most important job under financial stress but are being punished for that achievement by their accreditors.

Like taxes and death, government regulation and accreditation have been around for a very long time and are here to stay. Perhaps the game changer in recent decades is the ubiquitous advent of the Internet. Today, regulators publish all institutional "blemishes" or "shortfalls" on their website and often require the non-complying institution to follow suit by showcasing such shortfalls on its own websites.

Unfortunately, the way in which these infractions are presented often tends to amplify the negative in ways that can mislead the public into worrying that the institution being cited has chronic problems and should therefore be erased from the list of colleges under consideration for enrollment.

Despite all the amazing achievements of the Internet, the on-line publication of impediments (like mistakes in prosecuting and adjudicating Title IX date rape accusations, or accreditation assessments of relative financial health) tend to negate what in many cases is an overwhelming list of positives that pass unnoticed when such red flags are prominently displayed.

What to do about lawyers and compliance agencies is probably not a dilemma that any individual small private college can resolve. All of John Silber's recommendations, now over four decades old, have been disregarded and the problem in each of these sectors has worsened.

Rather than helping colleges solve these problems, lawyers and compliance regulators have taken on a near inquisitorial role that serves only to add often crippling burdens to already daunting challenges that colleges face in their attempts to secure their futures. To the contrary, both entities should be trying to help preserve the future of the national treasure that American higher education represents globally.

Thus, litigation from personal injury contingency lawyers, along with ominous statements from compliance agencies, have become top problems facing private higher education today. At some point, hopefully, the larger institutions with greater clout, along with national associations representing higher education will at least encourage these regulatory agencies to present a more balanced picture that also acknowledges what is right about the institution and thereby calling the glass half full instead of half empty, or worse.

America's colleges continue to be a national asset worthy of support, but a very large number of these institutions face daunting challenges.

Regulators should be trying to help our colleges overcome the daunting hurdles they face today instead of presenting additional costly and deferential hurdles.

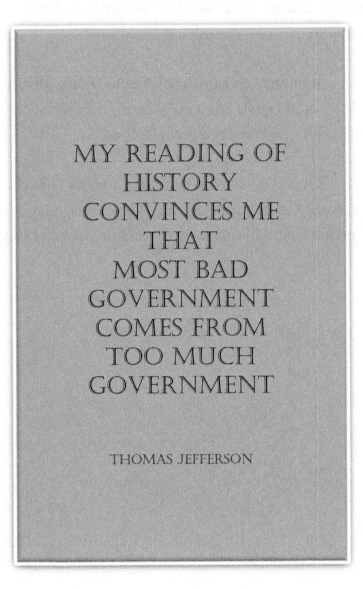

MY READING OF
HISTORY
CONVINCES ME
THAT
MOST BAD
GOVERNMENT
COMES FROM
TOO MUCH
GOVERNMENT

THOMAS JEFFERSON

In Closing

The sixteen problems comprising the chapters of this book clearly do not represent a comprehensive array of all issues and challenges facing all colleges and universities. Rather, these are what I believe to be the most usual "top," or prerequisite, problems that confront smaller, independent colleges heavily dependent on enrollment revenue. By prerequisite, I mean those problems that must first be resolved before more qualitative and ideological issues are addressed.

Of the approximately 2,000 private colleges in America, at least 75% are faced with one or more of these sixteen problems.

The more of these problems that burden any one college, the more urgent the need to move quickly and boldly. Many prognosticators forecast that hundreds of problem-ridden colleges will not survive, largely because of their inability to adapt.

The only real hope for any such challenged college is, in my view, for the Board of Trustees and the senior management to confront fiscal and managerial realities, even if the necessary changes will be unpopular which is almost inevitable. In many cases, a change in management and governance may well be required in order to provide new leadership capable of understanding and addressing these challenges.

Enrollment-revenue-dependent colleges must be managed more cost effectively, even if that should entail goring some long established sacred cows.

Enrollment-revenue-dependent colleges must realize that they cannot disregard the nuances of consumer behavioral traits common among families fortunate enough to have the financial resources to pay for higher tuition of a non-public (private/independent) college.

And, enrollment-revenue-dependent colleges have to avoid the temptations of emulating government-supported colleges and universities because it is financially impossible to successfully compete with publics for their students, especially if the schools are in close proximity to each other.

As Standard and Poor's 2017 prospectus for private higher education aptly observed, there is a viable place for independent higher education and many such colleges have never more flourished than today. At the same time, that many more such colleges have never faced more dire straits than today. Private higher education is bifurcated like never before.

Of important note is that the most successful private colleges and universities are the very ones not attempting to compete with public institutions. These flourishing institutions are also not being drawn into occupational programs that lead directly to a job, as former President Barack Obama advocated when he declared, in 2014, that "folks can make a lot more, potentially, with skilled manufacturing or the trades than they might with an art history degree," a statement he later retracted with regret.

Billionaire investor Mark Cuban is one of many who warn that skilled labor and trades are, to the contrary, in jeopardy of increasingly disappearing due to the rapid pace of automation. Like many of the most successful of his generation, Cuban believes the demand for broadly educated college graduates will grow, not shrink, in the years ahead.

A well-presented case for private colleges to stick with their DNA was authored by CNN and TIME magazine editor Fareed Zakaria, in his book titled "In Defense of a Liberal Education." In it, he observes that most college students are not drawn to such broad-based educational programs, but asserts that the most successful graduates continue to graduate from the colleges that maintain such a tradition of learning.

These same students come from families who recognize the life-time value of a core undergraduate experience that best prepares graduates for a lifetime of dynamic change to which they will have to confront and adapt. Those enlightened families tend to be parented by college graduates who themselves have found success, professionally and financially, and are thereby willing and able to pay what it costs for a first-rate college education for their children.

The private, enrollment-revenue-dependent colleges that will survive and flourish into the future are the ones that target those who are in the position to pay what it costs to underwrite the expenses of a private college or university experience. Chasing other prospects, in most cases, will prove an exercise in futility.

It all comes down to fiscal sustainability

which has to be the first-things-first, bite-the-bullet and smell-the-coffee focus of any private college that has any hope of a future. That said, it is an inconvenient truth that some private colleges will not have what it takes to compete and will therefore probably fail and close. Such fates have already befallen some colleges.

Those that survive, and, hopefully, flourish, will be those able to confront the issues and problems that include, first and foremost, the assembly of a governance and management team who work in tandem with each other.

This book has aspired to lay out the principal burdens facing colleges in the 'worst of worlds' portion of the bifurcated higher education sector described by Standard & Poor's in hopes that the road map to survival and prosperity is constructed.

IF
YOUR DREAMS
DON'T SCARE
YOU,
THEY
AREN'T
BIG
ENOUGH

MUHAMMAD ALI

&
OTHERS

IT TAKES A VILLAGE

T his book's theme, namely, the most daunting problems facing colleges today, compels me to close with an acknowledgment that, in respect to higher education, the glass is much more full than it is empty. Most noteworthy toward that end is array of inspiring people associated with the profession and the indelible role they play, from my first hand experience, in shaping the best of future generations. I have been fortunate, over the past five decades of my life in higher education, to be inspired by countless such people, the most indelible of which I cite here in chronological sequence beginning in the way back in the 1960's at Drexel University.

Drexel University

Oscar Eichhorn, Dean of Men
Lady Anne Foff Judge, Class of 1968
James Gallagher, Chair and Professor of Law
Fred Hawkins, Class of 1969
James McEwan, Chair and Professor of Marketing
C. R. Pennoni, President Emeritus & Chairman Emeritus
Martin Weinberg, Professor of Law & Deputy Mayor of Philadelphia
George Wilson, Asst. VP for Student Diversity
Stephen Lake Yale, Dean of Student Affairs

Philadelphia University

Patricia McGlone, Assistant to the Dean of Students
Barbara Moudy, Associate Dean of Students
Lawson & Marcia Pendleton, President & First Lady
Marianne Sobecki, Dirctor of Career Development

Harvard University

Derek Bok, President Emeritus, Harvard University
John Brademus, President Emeritus, New York University
Courtney Cazden, Professor of Teaching, Learning and Education
Michael Dukakis, Governor of Massachusetts & Kennedy School Director
Gardner Dunnan, Headmaster, The Dalton School
Bill Fitzsimmons, Dean of Admissions, Harvard University
Raymond Flynn, Kennedy School MPA & Mayor of Boston
Vernon Howard, Professor of Philosophy of Education
Harold Howe, Professor & US Commissioner of Education
Francis Keppel, Professor & US Commissioner of Education
Charles Kireker, Kennedy School of Government
Robert Klitgaard, Special Assistant to the President, Harvard University
Mary Murphy, Director of Admissions
Gregory Payne, Kennedy School MPA Professor, Emerson University
Jacqueline Roy, Director of Placement, Graduate School of Education
Rosemarie Sansone, Kennedy School MPA & Boston City Counselor
Israel Sheffler, Professor of Philosophy of Education
Stephen Trachtenberg, President Emeritus, The George Washington University
Ursula Wagener, Assistant Dean for Academic Affairs
Paul Ylvisaker, Dean of the Graduate School of Education

Wagner College

Tony Carter, Professor of Business
John Esser, Professor of Sociology

NORMAN R. SMITH

Wagner College

Bob Evans, Trustee & Benefactor
Robert Franek, Publisher, The Princeton Review
Miles Groth, Professor of Psychology
Lyle Guttu, College Chaplain & Asst. to the President
Donna Hanover, Trustee and First Lady New York City
Walt Hameline, Director of Athletics
Lewis Hardee, Professor of Theatre
Phil Hickox, Professor of Theatre
Fred Lange, Trustee & Benefactor
John Lehmann, Trustee & CEO of Butterick VOGUE
David Long, VP for External Relations
Judith Lunde, Assistant to the President
Martha Megerle, Trustee and Benefactor
Mildred Nelson, Associate Provost & Registrar
Bill and Peggy Reynolds, Trustees & Benefactors
Mordechai Rozanski, Provost
Anne Schotter, Professor of English Literature
Alison Smith, Professor of History
Constance Schuyler, Dean of Graduate Studies
Gary Sullivan, Chair of Performing and Visual Arts
Donald Spiro, Board Chair & CEO of Oppenheimer Funds

Richmond The American Int'l University in London

Professor Dominic Alessio, Director of Study Abroad Programs
Sir John Ashworth, Trustee & Head, London School of Economics
Lord (Richard) Attenborough of Richmond upon Thames, Presidential Advisor
Lord (Asa) Briggs of Lewes, Chair of Academic Governors
Sir Graeme Davies, Academic Governor and Vice Chancellor, U of London
Teresa Domzel, Provost & Dean of the School of Business
Jos Hackforth Jones, Provost & Presidential successor
Mark Kopenski, VP for Enrollment
David McAuliffe, Trustee and COO, JPMorgan London
Professor Agi Oldfield, School of Business
William Scott, VP for Administration and Finance

Richmond The American Int'l University in London

Wendy Stokes, Professor of Government
Russel Taylor, Trustee & Founder, Taylor Entrepreneurial Institute
Lord (Alan) Watson of Richmond, Trustee & Chair, English Speaking Union
Professor Christine Zaher, Dean of Academic Standards
Graham Zellick, Board Chair and Vice Chancellor, University of London

Alamein University, Egypt

Walid Abushakra, Trustee & Founder, ESOL
Joseph Jabbra, President, Lebanon American University

Dowling College

Tom Daly, Dean of Aviation
David Marker, Interim Provost
Clyde Payne, Vice President for Student Affairs
Deborah Richman, Trustee
Professor Nathalia Rogers, Chair of Faculty Council
Elana Zolfo, Dean of the School of Business

Suffolk University Boston

Daniel Conley, Trustee & Boston District Attorney
Leo Corcoran, Trustee & Urban Developer
Keri Cullinane, Executive Asst. to the Board of Trustees
Dan Esdale, Director of Marketing
Russell Gaudreau Esp., Trustee
Professor Kenneth Goldberg, Dean of Arts & Sciences
Tom Ingram, President Emeritus, Association of Governing Board
Marisa Kelly, Provost
Camille Nelson, Dean of the American University Law School
John Nucci, Sr. VP for External Relations

194

NORMAN R. SMITH

Suffolk University Boston

Bill O'Neil, Dean of the Business School
Andrew Meyer, Board Chair & Founder, Lubin & Meyer
Andrew Perlman, Dean of the Law School
Carol Sawyer Parks, Board Vice Chair & Benefactor
Richard Rosenberg, Trustee & CEO (ret) Bank of America
Bob Sheridan, Trustee & President Emeritus
Marshall Sloane, Trustee & Chairman, Century Bank
David Southworth, Trustee & President, Southworth Development

Elmira College

Mary Barret, Executive Asst. to the President
Bob Basel, Alumnus and Trustee
Bob Campe, VP for Administration & Finance
John Cardent, Alumnus and Trustee
Christopher Coons, VP for Enromment Management
Betsy Dalrymple, Trustee
Susanne Grennel, Alumna and Trustee
Tommy Hilfiger, Fashion Designer and Trustee
Karen Johnson, Director of Institutional Research
Charles & Janna Lindsay, Provost & successor first family
Doris Fischer Malesardi, Alumna and Trustee
Kathie Metzger, Board Vice Chair
Charlie Mitchell, Dean of Academic Affairs
Bob & Carol Morris, Board Chairman & Benefactors
Whitney Posillico, Alumna and Trustee
Michael Rogers, VP for External Relations
Patricia Thompson, VP for Athletics
Tom Tranter, Alumnus and Trustee
Clare van den Blink, Alumna and Trustee
Jack Walsh, Trustee
William Waldorf, Trustee
Franon Wilson, Trustee
George Winner, Trustee and former State Senator

195

STAMATS

STAMATS is, in my view, the gold standard for higher education marketing and branding, a critical facet in private college success today more than ever before. I have relied upon them for three decades at a number of the most successful college outcomes I have overseen as president and their role has been key to those successes.

Guy Wendler

President, has my gratitude and respect for assembling professional teams of the highest quality.

Marilyn Osweiler

Senior Vice President, is the best in her profession. I have relied upon her for projects dating back to the 1980's and she has always delivered outcomes that exceeded expectation. Her decades of clients throughout the US and internationally make her expertise invaluable. Marilyn played an important role in helping me assemble the issues presented in this book.

Chris Reese

Head Designer, is a visionary artist who has created and assembled some of the most head-turning marketing images that have ever been produced for colleges and universities. His work has been key to some of the most successful turnarounds I have ever come across or been a part of.

Jason Jones

STAMATS' go-to independent photographer is my choice for being viewed as the Ansel Adams of college and university photography. I don't know how he does it, but he makes colleges look their very best and even more than that. He creates images that make prospective students and their families want to visit and see for themselves.

www.stamats.com

THE REGISTRY

The Registry for College & University Presidents, which I cite and recommend in this book, is in 2017 celebrating 25 years of providing colleges and universities with interim senior leadership at not only the presidential level, but for deanships, vice preisdencies and other senior positions. After 25 years as a college president, I became a member. My most recent assignments, including Elmira College, have been interim projects via the Registry.

The Registry is headed by

George Matthews,

Chairman Emeritus of Northeastern University and my co-author of
WHAT COLLEGE TRUSTEES NEED TO KNOW.

Bryan Carlson

is the Registry's President and my co-author of
WHAT COLLEGE TRUSTEES NEED TO KNOW.

Kevin Matthews

Vice President

Amy Lauren Miller

Vice President

Jacqueline Armitage

Vice President

www.registryinterim.com

Published in 2013. Available from
on-line book retailers including
bookstore.iuniverse.com,
Barnes & Noble and Amazon.com.

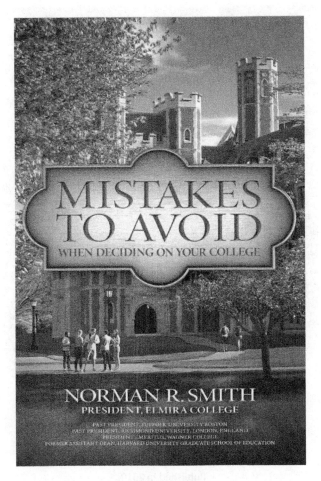

Published in 2016.
Written for high school college counselors and
college bound students and their families.
Available for free download at www.elmira.edu
and at www.normansmith.org.

Published in 2010.
A chronicle of the turnaround years for Wagner College
when a near bankrupt institution facing closure
evolved into a flourishing TIME magazine "College of the Year."
Available from on-line book retailers including
bookstore.iuniverse.com,
Barnes & Noble & Amazon.com

Originally published in 1994 and reprinted annually through 2000, book is now out of print, but updated in the retitled "Mistakes to Avoid." Book is periodically offered for resale at ebay.com.

To contact the author,
go to

www.normansmith.org

CPSIA information can be obtained
at www.ICGtesting.com
Printed in the USA
BVOW09*1504120517
483763BV00001B/1/P